Crack the Spine
XVIII

Edited by Kerri Farrell Foley

Collection Copyright © 2019 Crack the Spine

ISBN 978-1-7328693-1-8

Individual works are the sole property of the authors.

Published by Crack the Spine Literary Magazine
Printed in the United States of America

Crack the Spine Literary Magazine
Houston, Texas ~ Galveston, Texas
www.crackthespine.com

Table of Contents

Larry Duncan

Uncertain Victory

"Is it wrong," she asked,
"to wipe my whiskey
hands on your jeans?"

"Not on a denim like today,"
I answered, neither one
knowing what we meant,
she having already chewed
the straw in a half empty
glass down to the lip,
and I having just sat
down for lunch.

But the laughter came
easy all the same,
pure enough to raise a few heads
on the other side of the bar
before silence settled back in.

Her husband returned
from a piss and they left.
Still, the afternoon light
turned a bit brighter,
and the same jukebox
songs seemed new.

I ordered another round,
Bushmills and a chaser,
deciding to drink
the rest of the afternoon
enough for us both.

Larry Duncan currently lives in Redondo Beach, CA. His poetry has appeared in *Juked*, the *Mas Tequila Review*, the *Redshift Anthology*, the *Free State Review* and John Grochalski's *Shipwrecked in Trumpland* Blog. He is the author of two chapbooks, *Crossroads of Stars and White Lightning* and *Drunk on Ophelia*.

Just Desserts

"Miss Teen USA? Hmm. Sure. What does one cite in a recommendation letter for a Miss Teen USA candidate?"

"It is a pageant however it's also about academic aptitude. That's why I need recommendations from my high school teachers. The pageant administrator told me that I scored higher on the academic testing than any candidate ever had," I replied to Mr. Cohan, my Spanish teacher.

"Why don't you meet me on the corner after dark, near the pizzeria, and we can discuss it. Let's say around 6pm," he said looking down at the Spanish exams on his desk.

"Ah, OK." I had to stay after school anyway for "Sing" rehearsal, though I did think he would just agree right there and then like Mr. Nelson, my English teacher, did. *Perhaps I should have asked Miss Mar instead of Mr. Cohan*, I thought.

All during "Sing" rehearsal, I kept thinking I hope he agrees to write the letter so I could finish the application. The whole thing was so fraught. My father had warned, "A Jewish girl is never going to win. You're just setting yourself up for failure."

"But, Dad, Bess Myerson won Miss America in 1945 and she's Jewish. I really want that scholarship money."

"Myerson's win is an anomaly," Dad said. "No Jewish New York teen is going to win in a pageant held in the heart of Texas."

During WWII, other U. S. Air Force men had harassed for being Jewish. "Where are your horns?" one soldier remarked, someone who had never seen a Jew before. Dad told me the rabid anti-Semitism forced him to challenge many a fellow airman.

"You can go to Queens College, down the block. You don't need that scholarship money—your state merit scholarship would cover the cost of a city college," Dad said.

About to leave my mother for good, Dad had one foot out the door of our home and wasn't about to fork up whatever money was needed to buy the pageant dresses and other stuff. Besides, if I were to attend the local college, I would live at home with my mother, making him feel freer, I surmised. My exemplary test scores and dance talent routine had my mother convinced I had a shot at the title. Mom gathered every dime she had ever saved; she said, "Just don't tell Daddy until we're there. OK, my girl?"

Leaning on a small, green car, smoking a cigarette, Mr. Cohan was waiting on the corner.

"Hi, Mr. Cohan."

He nodded a hello back and put out his cigarette. "Get in. Let's take a ride. And then I'll drive you home."

I never had been inside such a small car; I only had seen a VW Beetle in LIFE magazine ads. I felt too closed in— though the scent of cigarettes, after shave and old coffee cups was kind of grossly intoxicating. My father smoked but our car never smelled and neither did Daddy. Mr. Cohan shut the passenger side door.

Driving and clutching the gearshift, he spoke, "So tell me about this pageant. Why do you want to do it? I didn't think smart girls entered beauty pageants. And, oh yeah, if this is Miss Teen USA, does that mean you're already Miss Teen New York?"

"I *am* Miss New York Teen USA, 1970; yes. I need the scholarship money. First prize is $5,000. I want to attend a private university—the one my friends are applying to—and my parents only can afford public college. I want to be a painter."

"You are very beautiful," he said clearing his throat. "OK. Sure, I'll write the letter for you. And since you need money, I'll set up an interview for you with a friend of mine who is an attorney. He probably could use a smart, attractive young woman as a receptionist during the summer. Interested?"

"Thank you very much, Mr. Cohan. I appreciate your help. Do you think you could drop me off on the boulevard, please? I have to get back home. My mother is going to worry about me."

"Let's just drive a bit longer. I want to hear more about you so I can write the letter."

He drove for what seemed like an awfully long time. Finally, he stopped at a light. "I'll just get out here," I said, flinging the car door open as he reached for me.

"Today we're going to conjugate verbs. Conjugating verbs involves changing a verb form…" he walked past my desk and slipped a piece of paper on the desk along with the graded exam. "Meet me. Same place, same time."

Bile seemed to fill my throat.

"Can someone tell me the different meanings of the verb, *querer*?"

Mr. Cohan called on Peter.

"Yes, Pedro. Very good. You are correct—it means both 'to want' and 'to love'," said Mr. Cohan, who had assigned a Spanish name to each of us in the class.

Though he had always called on me in the past, Mr. Cohan avoided looking at me during the entire class and never called on me again, which was fine because I detested my assigned name, "Rosita."

I was unprepared for 6pm.

There he was again, leaning on his Beetle. As I approached, he dropped his cigarette to the pavement and put it out with his scuffed loafer. "Hop in—I'll take you for ice cream."

"I am hoping you'll write the letter," I said, hesitating to get into his car. My body stiffened.

Why did you get into that car you stupid girl? Why didn't you ask Miss Mar instead?

He touched my hand, directing me into the car, "Feel like ice cream or talking somewhere private?"

I did like Mr. Cohan. He was intense, kind of handsome, and not really old, not as old as my parents at least. Maybe that's why I asked him; I knew he favored me. *Maybe it was all my fault.*

I didn't have my driver's license yet so I didn't know where he was heading, taking all those back streets. Next thing I know we were parked in back of the Par Central Motor Inn. "Wait here, in the car. I'll be right back," he said. "They have good ice cream here."

"But...but..." He didn't hear me.

He returned in a few minutes with Good Humor ice cream pops and a room key. *Why did I go into that room?*

June rolled around. Everyone was signing yearbooks. He wrote in mine:

"Te quiero.

Te quiero más.

Te quiero más que mi vida.

Que más querés?

Querés más?"*

6

Lucy, my old bandmate from high school, friends me on Facebook. In the school band, she had been second clarinet; I was third clarinet, though I barely deserved that distinction. Lucy's hair always was meticulously teased up high on her head with a tiny bow adorning the part between her bangs and big hair. Using her clarinet mouthpiece, she had shown me how to give a blow job during one band class. I always found her experience exciting. Lucy also was my classmate in Spanish and Hygiene classes. During Hygiene classes, she'd always ask the most daring questions just to rile our ultra-conservative teacher, who we referred to as Miss Cobwebs. Using Facebook Messenger, we catch up on our respective lives. Husbands. Children. Work. Hobbies. We both have only daughters.

"What's your number? I want to hear your voice—for old times' sake," Lucy says and then calls a few seconds later.

"Hey Lucy, are you in touch with any of our teachers from high school?" *Are any on Facebook? Any alive?* I wonder. It's been forty years and I had never attended any H.S. reunions. "I often think fondly of Mr. Garo and his baton, even though he didn't let me try out for the sax or drums. 'Boys only for those instruments, Missy,' he'd said," I imitate his deep voice.

"Didn't you just hate Miss Cobwebs? What a prude!" Lucy says. Her voice still sounds like honey to me, but suddenly, the blood rushes from my head as it does from time to time when I flash back. Curious how that same dizzying physical response often precedes that repeated feeling of dread. With the flood of daily stories in the news, I have to work really hard to push down the surges.

"Do you know whatever happened to our Spanish teacher?" I ask though I can't even bring myself to utter his name.

"Funny—I went to visit my Aunt Gertie, my mother's older sister who is in a nursing home on Long Island, and I see this man who looks familiar to me. So, I walk over to him, you know me, and look closer. I look right into his face. And it's him—it's Mr. Cohan!"

"Did you talk to him?" I ask, as my stomach hollows.

"Of course, I did. I said to him, 'Hey, Mr. Cohan. Remember me? It's me, Lucy, I mean, Lucia, from Spanish class at John Brown High?'"

"Did he remember you?"

"Well, I do look different. No more bows in my hair," she giggles. "But I kind of think he did. He didn't say anything, just smiled," Lucy says.

"Where's the nursing home?"

"It's in Long Beach—Belle Air Retirement. Ha! Not really a retirement home—more like a 'waiting until death' home. They're all kind of out of it, there, if you know what I mean," Lucy says.

"That is a coincidence, about your Aunt and all. I really enjoyed catching up. Take care, Lucy." I wonder if she could hear my tone change.

That last bit of conversation took my day and put it in the shitter. Now all I can think of is what I should have done differently. "You can call me, 'Moe,'" he had said that early evening. "I will definitely introduce you to my friend, Isadore, the Wall St. attorney. Wait until he gets a load of you!"

I head to the kitchen to look for a Dramamine.

When I had gone for the interview at the Wall Street office, everyone was matter of fact. "Let's hear how you would answer the phone?" "Can you take a message?"

Paula, their receptionist, was going away for a month-long vacation so they needed a temp. "You come highly recommended by Mr. Levy's friend," Paula said. She winked at me. "Everyone here is nice enough considering it's Wall Street." Paula laughed, and then continued in a whisper, "Except for Mr. Gray, the senior partner, and Mr. Levy."

"Here's $3." Paula took money from an envelope marked "petty cash." "When you start tomorrow morning, stop off and buy a corn muffin and light and sweet coffee for Mr. Levy. Believe me that's the only 'light and sweet' thing about him," Paula said.

I knocked on his door. "Good morning, Mr. Levy. Here's your breakfast," I said. It was 8am and he was working already. He didn't look up. No response.

I answered phones. In between calls, I hadn't been assigned any tasks so I was reading, *The Feminine Mystique*, my new bible.

"Where's Paula?" I heard someone ask. I looked up from my book and it was Mr. Levy, who towered over my desk.

"Paula is on vacation," I replied.

"Oh, right. You're the girl Moe sent? How old are you?" he didn't really expect a reply, I figured from his facial expression.

"I was placed into the academically gifted programs and skipped two grades, just like Carole King, so I will graduate high school at sixteen…"

He cut me off, "I hope you have working papers."

I started to reply but Mr. Levy spoke again, "Did Moe tell you anything about me?"

"Just that you're his friend, an attorney, and needed a receptionist for the summer. I'm earning money for college."

"There are opportunities here to earn extra money," he said. "I'll be back in an hour."

The first day wasn't so bad though I had to take messages for five of the six partners in the law firm. The senior partner, Mr. Gray, had a private receptionist slash personal assistant. All of the partners were bald and stuffed into their pin-striped suits, except for Mr. Levy, who was slim with slicked-back, black, wavy hair. They treated me as if I were an answering machine—there but not there. The partners were polite and robotic. Some asked for small favors, such as going downstairs to the neighborhood shops to buy coffee or pick up their dry cleaning. Some would tip me. "This is for the extra trouble," one would say. "Here's five bucks, kid." Errands were a chance to earn extra money and get out of the beige office space. All through the day, I hoped for tips, and silently would recite a couple of lines from an English folk rhyme I had recalled from grammar school,

"I knock at the knocker, I ring the little bell.

Please give me, then, a penny, for singing this so well."

It seemed Mr. Levy only expected his breakfast and messages.

During the first week, I had gotten a lot of reading done and managed to sneak in a phone call to my mother. Two weeks. Then three flew by. I read most of the freshman year reading list for the university I hoped to attend. *The Bluest Eye. Islands in the Stream. Portnoy's Complaint.*

"Take six dollars from petty cash for tomorrow and buy yourself breakfast, too," Mr. Levy said as he walked in and past my desk.

"OK. Thank you." I sure could use the three bucks.

Four o'clock rolled around quickly. "Before you leave, stop into my office," Mr. Levy said to me.

"I am entertaining two clients from Korea. Do you have any friends who would want to meet them?" he asked.

My eyes popped, "No. I don't believe I do."

"How about you accompany me, then? There's twenty-five dollars in it for you."

"Excuse me? Twenty-five dollars to accompany you and your clients to dinner?" I asked.

"Yes. Exactly. My wife is away and I need arm candy to impress them."

I had never heard that expression before.

He took his wallet out of his suit pocket. "Here's $100. Go buy a new dress, shoes, have your hair done, and meet me back here at 7pm," Mr. Levy said, even though I hadn't even responded affirmatively.

At 7pm, I had to sign into the building. "Meeting Mr. Levy," I wrote in the log.

He took my elbow. "Let's go. We're meeting them at a Korean restaurant a couple of blocks away." I hurried in my new heels.

The next day was as usual. "Here's your muffin and coffee, Mr. Levy." No response. By four o'clock, I put down *The Second Sex*. Looking down, I began to sort the pink paper messages, get rid of the blank ones I doodled on, and tidy the reception area. I laughed to myself, *When I'm a famous artist those doodles might be worth something.*

"Why do you read that feminist trash?" Mr. Levy asked standing over my desk.

"I'm a feminist," I said.

"Oh really."

"Really. I said. I'm a liberated woman—I can do whatever men can do. I'm going to study at a great university and be an artist like Georgia O'Keefe," I replied. Little did I know I got feminism kind of screwed up back then.

"Meet me tonight at the same restaurant, Miss Liberated," he said. "In 30 minutes for happy hour."

"Ah, I don't drink. I told you that last night."

"That's OK. Arm candy, remember?"

We sat at the restaurant bar waiting for his clients. "So, it has come to my attention that this is your last week at our office," he said, as he held up his glass for a toast. "Good luck to you," he toasted.

"Thanks. I appreciate the job, Mr. Levy," I said.

"Now that you won't be working for us anymore, call me 'Isadore'," he said and ordered another drink. I had never met someone who drank so much liquor. My father had an occasional scotch when company came over. "You've been great—smarter with clients than Paula, our regular girl. For that, I'm going to confer a bonus." He pulled hundred dollar bills out of his wallet. I had never seen a one hundred-dollar bill before. "Here's $400—one hundred for every week you worked for the firm. And I'll need your assistance one more night. Tomorrow night. OK?"

"Gee, thanks for the bonus. Tomorrow is my last day. Uh, OK, I guess. Another clients' dinner with Mr. Park and Mr. Kim? They are formidable…"

He cut me off, "Just meet me at the St. Regis bar at 7pm. Wear the same dress you wore last night."

Not sure how someone who is so school smart could be so stupid otherwise. Would fate be so kind to me as to put Levy in the same nursing home as Cohan?

I get off the Long Island Railroad and hail a taxi. On the road, I think of my conversation earlier in the week with Lucy who asked, "Hey, wait…did you ever go to Texas? Did you win Miss Teen USA?"

"I didn't go to Texas so I had to forfeit my Miss New York Teen title to the runner up. Long story, Lucy, better told over a glass of wine. Let's just say I'm a survivor."

I enter the nursing home. "Hello, I'm here to see Moe Cohan. I'm his niece," I say to the Belle Air Retirement home receptionist, whose silver nameplate reads, "Dolores."

"Oh, how lovely. He rarely gets visitors. He'll be so happy to see you. He's having dinner right now. After your uncle has had his chocolate cake, I can arrange for you to have a visit. He sure loves his chocolate cake—he waits for that all day," the receptionist tells me.

"Can I just peak into the dining room, Dolores?"

"Well, I don't see why not," Dolores replies. "Right over there, hon."

I walk in. No one stops me. I look around to see if I can spot him. There he is.

I push back retching.

Before I leave, I ask the receptionist, "Dolores, will you be on duty tomorrow night?"

"My night off and boy do I need it!" she says. "This place can wear out your soul."

As Dolores turns her back, I scurry out.

The next evening, I return to the Belle Air Retirement Home. Lucky for me it is indeed Dolores' night off. "Hello, I'm here to see Moe Cohan's health attendant. His niece was here yesterday—you can check with Dolores. I'm the dietician his niece engaged," I say to Kamila, the Belle Air Retirement home receptionist.

"Sure. I'll call Mr. Cohan's attendant. Your name, please?"

"Ms. Rosita," I reply.

Mr. Cohan's Belle Air Retirement home attendant appears. Pink uniform, plump rosy cheeks with hair pinned back, she looks like someone out of a Botero painting. "Hello. I'm Ms. Rosita, the dietician Moe Cohan's niece engaged," I say to her. "Do you arrange his meals and snacks?" I ask her.

"Yes, indeedy! I do. Nice to meet ya."

"Thank you, Charlene. May I call you Charlene? Yes, nice to meet you, too. Ah, so, Mr. Cohan's niece is concerned about his diabetes. And I'm sure you don't want to rush his demise or have him loose a leg because he's having too much sugar."

"Oh, goodness me, no. I didn't see that info on his chart," Charlene replies with her mouth now taking on a sour shape.

"His niece says he's a smooth talker—he probably convinced the admitting attendant to omit that information. You know how some diabetics minimize the adverse effects of sugar on their condition. But, Charlene, I'm here to tell you he may *not* have any desserts, especially chocolate cake."

Charlene looks at her wristwatch. "Oh, my!" she says. Abruptly, she turns and heads towards the dining hall. I follow. I stop as she rushes to a nearby table. Looking in, I see him, Mr. Cohan with fork in hand. I watch as Charlene takes away his dessert.

*English translation:

"I want you.

I want you more.

I love you more than my life.

What more do you want?

What more?"

Disclaimer: The story, all names, characters, and incidents portrayed in this work are fictitious. No identification with actual persons (living or deceased), places, buildings, motels, or nursing homes is intended or should be inferred.

Robin holds the title of Distinguished Professor at Kean University and she is the author of 23 published nonfiction books and a children's book. Robin has won numerous awards for design, writing and research, including awards from the *National Society of Arts and Letters* and the *National League of Pen Women*. She received the 2015 *Human Rights Educator* award, 2013 *Kean Teacher of the Year*, and the *Carnegie Foundation* lists Robin among the great teachers of our time.

Ryan Curcio

Balt's Birthday Nightmare

Balt Crick sat in the sparsely furnished waiting room of a mental health clinic, reading last month's copy of Sports Illustrated for Kids. He shifted in his lime green chair and, as he did this, it made a sound resembling a fart. The receptionist's face wrinkled into a grimace, and the hairy mole on her chin tightened into the shape of an earth-worm. Just as Balt went to explain the source of the noise, she slid the small, plastic window shut.

Five minutes later, the receptionist cracked the window open, revealing only a sliver of space, in the event the smell of Balt's imaginary fart still lingered, and yelled out with her nose plugged, "Mr. Creeeick, Dr. Rolllland weeeill seeee you naaaaw."

She shut the window the second the last syllable left her tongue. Balt stood up and walked through the door separating the psychoanalyzed from those waiting to be psychoanalyzed. Balt was sweating profusely. His bald patch shone under the fluorescent lighting; his last session with Dr. Roland had been highly unproductive.

Balt turned the fat silver knob of Dr. Roland's office door and walked in to see the doctor seated in a large leather armchair.

"Balt! How are you feeling today? Take a seat, please. Sorry you had to wait an extra few minutes. I was with Mrs. Stockton and she wouldn't stop yammering about her pet ostri—oh wait, I'm not supposed to tell you that. Doctor-patient confidentiality—that whole bit," he chuckled softly. "I recall that at the end of our last session, I told you to go home and think of a significant moment, one from your childhood that really stood out in shaping who you are today. Good or bad. Have you given that any thought, Balt?"

Balt stared down at the complex geometrical pattern on the carpet with unblinking eyes, "Yes I have, actually. It's a moment I think I can attribute to a lot of the anxiety issues I have. I think it really ruined my self confidence…Tragic stuff," Balt added pensively.

Dr. Roland leaned back in his chair, then rocked forward, "Well that's my specialty, Balt. Go ahead and lay it on me."

Balt sighed and scratched hard behind his ear, "Okay, here goes. When I turned six years old, my mom made me have a birthday party. There was a bounce-house, many colorful balloons, streamers, the works. My mother insisted on there being a clown to perform at the party, but I am petrified of their very presence. The clown behaved more like a mime, because he wouldn't say anything, and he kept following me around with a cigarette hanging out of his toothless mouth. What happened next still haunts me to this day. My father kicked our back glass door until it shattered, little shards scattering all over the patio. He had just returned from his third shift job, and obviously had done some drinking on the way home. He started pushing my little friends to the grass—parents were screaming at him the whole time—and he began gorging out on all the food. Little bits of chicken were flying everywhere, he drank all the Kool-Aid, and he devoured more than half of a party size pizza. I started to cry and tugged at his work trousers, begging him to stop. No one else wanted to go near him. He had gotten into the cake now, and turned to look at me with glazed eyeballs, his lips blue from the frosting. He spit little chunks of cake out on my face as he said this, but I'll never forget the words, 'You don't deserve a birthday party and you don't deserve a birthday either! I never wanted a kid. I wanted to travel the world and be a professional competitive eater. Mistake!' he roared, and went stumbling over to the bounce-house to sleep it off. Kids were screaming after he flopped down on the floor of the bounce-house— the scabbard of his hunting knife must have had a hole in it, because the bounce-house started to deflate."

After Balt finished speaking, he pressed his palms to his face, covering up his eyes. Dr. Roland's eyes were the size of half dollars, and his mouth looked as if the Jaws of Life had pried his lips apart. He looked at his smart watch, and said, "Oh my, I am so sorry Balt. I actually need to go. My wife just texted me—she has a terrible case of hemorrhoids, you understand—and I need to get over to the pharmacy to pick up her prescription for an ointment to deal with the discomfort. Once again, I'm *so* sorry."

Balt's eyebrows rose to his hairline, and he replied, "But couldn't you just get something over the coun—"

Doctor Roland held a hand up, and said, "No, I'm afraid over the counter won't do. She'll develop anal fissures if I don't get her this very potent, medical brand only available through prescription. You will of course not be expected to pay the full amount for today's visit, so I will cut off twenty five percent of your session's cost. The *least* I can do. Now, I really must be running."

The doctor put on his coat and ushered Balt out of his office.

Balt stood in the street for a moment, then reached into his pocket for something. It was a slice of birthday cake—enclosed in a Ziploc baggy—his mother had baked for him earlier. He turned forty-six that day.

Ryan Curcio is a senior at Central Connecticut State University. He studies English with a minor in Writing. He was a contributing writer for Trill! Magazine, and acted as an intern reporter for the New Britain Herald. His work has appeared in undergraduate literary magazines, on 121words.com, The Wagon Magazine, and Crack the Spine. He was a finalist for the Leslie Leeds Poetry Prize in 2018.

Jesse Minkert

Texas, 1952

I stitched together this fragment of the past much like a quilt, from actual memories, stories, and what I inferred from combinations of the two.

First, the place. Brazos County, Texas, occupies the triangle of land between the Brazos and Navasota Rivers. The city of Bryan shares a boundary with College Station and Texas A&M University.

Now a memory. I am four years old, and I hear my father and mother scream at each other through the wall between my bedroom and theirs. In the daylight, their voices keep even. The only sign of discord is the distance between them. No embraces, no pats on the shoulder, no handholding, no quick, peck-like kisses, no apparently accidental brushes of hip against hip, no physical contact of any kind. I'm far too young to notice something missing I've never seen, but I can feel the repelling force, like what happens when I try to push the north poles of two magnets together.

Once the house lights are out, their hostility is less ambiguous. Their words are blurred, either by the walls or by the insulation of decades, because I can't tell you now exactly what they said. But the content is clear. The marriage is a ring of hell; a battleground from which neither one can walk away. All of this happened every night of every year I lived in that house, which was roughly nineteen.

The house is in a yard, and the yard is vast. A giant A-frame swing of rusty pipe competes with a huge live oak for domination of the back. The side yards flank the steeply roofed, story-and-a-half, clapboard bunker in which we eat and sleep. The front is a flat expanse of Saint Augustine green, punctured by the branchless trunk of a dead tree by the walk.

Now comes a section I don't remember, but heard from them and they told to others in my presence many times.

I am not allowed to leave the yard, but I do. Maybe I want time and distance away from them and their unrelenting tension, or I feel no compulsion to obey their rules, since they can't agree on any rules between themselves that don't go away every night, or they're right when they tell me I'm the source of everything wrong with the family. All speculation, of course. I don't know why I felt compelled to leave the yard.

When I step out of my mother's field of vision, she launches a drama that plays without variation uncountable times. Here is approximately how it goes:

"He's been hit by a car! A pervert's got him! Find him!"

She whips Dad and my older sister into a frenzy. They search, and Mother's shrill voice calls my name. They find me, invariably in a neighbor's yard on the same block. I'm not hiding.

They bring me home, but Mother's screams don't stop. My father, desperate to calm her down, takes off his belt and beats me. My sister begs him to stop. Eventually Mother calms down, and he stops.

Again and again, I leave the yard. Again and again, my father's belt strikes me. Frustrated by their inability to force a four-year-old into submission with pain, my parents cast about for an alternative.

The next time, they take off my clothes and put a diaper on me. My father holds me up to the big, round mirror on the dresser. That's a memory. I can see that reflection to this day.

"If you act like a baby," my mother says, "we'll dress you like one."

My father puts me down, and I dive under the bed. Dad reaches for me; Mother gets hysterical. Hours pass before I come out.

Still, they got what they wanted. I never left the yard again.

Authority triumphed. All was well at last.

They were so impressed with the results of this new method of child control by humiliation, in the years that followed, they took every occasion to tell the story of how they returned balance to the universe with a diaper. They told it, in my presence, to relatives, to acquaintances, and to strangers. The story entered the family archive of stories. With each telling, the villain, that defiant child who refused to be beaten into submission, was painted in darker colors, and the parental brilliance of switching to psychological warfare appeared more creative and, at the same time, unavoidable.

And the people who listened nodded, and smiled, and said nothing.

It's different now. They're dead, and I'm the storyteller.

I have a supplementary tale in which I do not behave at my best, but which fills a gap I feel a need to fill. This I remember in every detail.

I'm in my teens, in the living room with my younger sister. I walk past her, and for some reason I put my hand on her neck. She says nothing. I go on my way.

Mother comes screaming at me. She says, because of me, my sister lost consciousness. Mother slaps me as hard as she can. My father takes off his belt. I stand in their bedroom, and he swings it at the backs of my legs. My knees buckle under the pain.

I am horrified at what I'd done to my sister. I'd endure any punishment they had for me. However, the pain wakes something up. It's not a memory. I reach back through the years to offer a degree of respect for the four-year-old I'd been, who'd taken so many of these lashes, yet wouldn't bend.

Jesse Minkert lives in Seattle. In 2008, Wood Works Press published a letterpress chapbook of his microfiction, *Shortness of Breath & Other Symptoms*. His work has appeared in over seventy journals including *the Cream City Review, Confrontation, Mount Hope, the Floating Bridge Review, the Minetta Review, Poetry Northwest, Common Knowledge, and Harpur Palate.* Thanks to *Raven Chronicles*, he is a 2016 Pushcart Nominee. In 2017, Finishing Line Press published his poetry chapbook, *Rookland*.

Jeff Fleischer

Father's Wishes

His last request was that we shouldn't bury him on the sabbath. We knew the law said to finish before sunset, but he wanted the family mourning in temple. We obliged, even as it meant his body sat overnight.

The frost came while we slept, and by morning the ground was too hard to dig. For hours, we took our spades and shovels to the unforgiving earth, until our muscles strained and we gave up. It took three days' toil before we could lay our father to rest.

Our next trip to temple was to ask forgiveness for our failure.

Jeff Fleischer is a Chicago-based author, journalist and editor. His fiction has appeared in more than two dozen publications including the *Chicago Tribune's Printers Row Journal*, *Shenandoah*, the *Saturday Evening Post* and *So It Goes* by the Kurt Vonnegut Memorial Library. He is also the author of non-fiction books including *Votes of Confidence: A Young Person's Guide to American Elections* (Zest Books, 2016), *Rockin' the Boat: 50 Iconic Revolutionaries* (Zest Books, 2015), and *The Latest Craze: A Short History of Mass Hysterias* (Fall River Press, 2011). He is a veteran journalist published in *Mother Jones*, the *New Republic*, the *Sydney Morning Herald*, the *Chicago Tribune*, *Chicago Magazine*, *Mental_Floss*, *National Geographic Traveler* and dozens of other local, national and international publications.

A.R. Robins

Bird Watching

There are birds on the television

The kitten has invented a game. She bats the TV with her downy feet at their smug bird faces.

I've invented a game too—it's bird word association for perverts.

Barn Swallow=Farmgirl Porn Name

Brown-headed Nuthatch= Chocolate Banana with Chicken Eggs

Tufted Titmouse=Too Easy

My best friend's mother-in-law posted on Facebook "I love hummers <3" I was drinking tea and scratching my head at the emoji comments—the eggplant is clever, but why not the cucumber, the corn, the carrot, or the baguette? Perhaps the peanut —

In second grade I called a kid a pecker-head, and my teacher wrote a note to my mother.

When my mother looked at me with her red head and white breast, I realized that what I had said had nothing to do with a boy with a wood-pecker face, and I was too afraid to ask.

A.R. Robins received her M.A. at Southeast Missouri State University. Her fiction has been published in *Potomac Review, Moon City Review, Opossum, The Big Muddy, The Swamp,* and others. Her poetry has been published in *Trailer Park Quarterly, The Cape Rock, Atlas and Alice,* and others. She currently lives in Missouri with her husband, son, and two cats.

R. Daniel Evans

Of Bacchus and Bulls

Elaine set up a tall canvas on her easel. Merce Cunningham, the dancer, would soon ring the doorbell. Though challenging, Elaine decided a full length portrait of his entire body seemed to be the best way to paint him. It would be another in her series of people she knew and liked. A dancer would have a lithe body, and she smiled at the thought of how she used to loathe anatomy class in art school. Now all those days of struggling with skeleton and flayed figure drawings would pay off.

Merce rang the doorbell and soon she heard his steps on the four flights. He had a quirky smile and greeted her with a chaste kiss on the cheek. After all, he was one of those Village types who only slept with other men. What did it matter? All the bullshit against fairies by Bill and Pollock was just to boost their own male egos, Elaine thought. Merce, easy to get along with, chatted about his choreography, and how happy he was to be free of dancing with Martha Graham. Meanwhile, she moved his limbs this way and that, finally coming to a pose that struck some sort of chord about his shy grace and how much he could control his body.

It took the rest of the afternoon just to sketch in some charcoal outlines on the canvas—how large to make the figure in relationship to the surrounding space, what to emphasize in his face and his torso. It seemed he could hold the pose for a long time without complaining, unlike most models. But naturally that's what dancers did, follow instructions perfectly. At the end of the session, he promised to come back the next day.

After he left, Elaine thought about some of the other people she'd painted. Then she drew Merce's figure the way she remembered it, without looking at the canvas. She sat and sketched with her back to the wind as it crept through the broken window. Her thoughts circled back to Bill. Her friends had been foolish to complain about de Kooning being fourteen years older than her. What did it matter? Now he was her mentor, her teacher, her lover. What other Dutchman had wanted to become an American simply because he admired Gorky, Stuart Davis and other abstract painters? She thought of his handsome square face, his broad, bull-like shoulders and the prematurely white hair with bangs that flipped off his head, first right then left, like a wide paint brush dancing on a canvas. His looks were so different from hers, nothing at all like her haunted dark eye sockets, narrow jaw and perpetually turned-down lips which she revealed in her self portrait. They would always be a peculiar couple, no matter how many years they might spend together. She knew he loved her, he had told her so, even though he could be bossy and demanding. Elaine enjoyed hearing him talk about art, the challenges artists faced, and the artists he admired.

She guessed that the room in the walk-up would remain sparse for some time. Even with the lowest rents in a run-down section of the city, down by the Bowery, they still couldn't afford any furniture other than stuff they found discarded on the sidewalks. But she would make an effort to court the critic Harold Rosenberg on Bill's behalf. She liked Harold, and if Bill gained recognition, the gallery could sell his works. Elaine loved him and wanted him to succeed, to become famous.

Suddenly, Bill walked into the apartment. "Christ, where's the coffee?"

"Over on the stove." With a stick of charcoal, Elaine pointed to a corner.

Bill slammed the pot on a counter. "It's cold. Can't you keep the burner lit when you know I'll be home soon? And I guess we're out of booze, right?"

She nodded, stood and then grabbed a match to relight the gas burner. "I'll reheat the coffee. Did you talk to that gallery dealer?"

He pivoted, then slapped the air. "Let's not talk about it. What did you do this afternoon?"

"More sketches. Some still life objects, my face, those glasses on the table."

"Let me see them," Bill said impatiently.

She held out her sketch book. He turned the pages, sometimes fast, sometimes slowly. "You haven't been listening to what I've told you. You have to combine precision of line with the grand sweep of your pencil. You can do better."

"These are weak," Bill continued. "Let's get rid of them." He tore up some pages and stuffed them into the garbage bin.

Elaine's mouth fell open, but she didn't say a word. At least he had already sold some of his paintings, and she thought him a great artist. So maybe he could teach her more about drawing.

She had already painted a partially blurred portrait of Bill, and one of Fairfield Porter, with his legs stretched wide apart, despite the fact his suit and tie looked more than respectable. Like her, Porter was not only an artist, but also a critic, one she admired. She had mixed emotions about writing reviews. Someone in their art 'Club' had to promote important living artists like Bill, Pollock, and the others. Poet Frank O'Hara wrote short critical pieces, and so did Fairfield Porter. But it wasn't enough. Elaine then thought of her portrait of O'Hara. It showed a standing figure, and she liked the way she had captured Frank's arrogance and self-possession, an attitude revealed by his bold stance, confronting the world, and even by his freely-painted white pants, done in broad brushstrokes. At the last minute Elaine had decided that the face didn't resemble him, and had blotted it out with a bright splotch of pink paint, like a bandage slapped on him by an angry celestial being. Even such a bandage couldn't stop Frank's outrageous chatter about his own life and everyone else's. Poets usually didn't talk about themselves. When she had painted Allen Ginsberg, he had sat in his Buddhist pose on the floor and had chanted his own poetry and William Blake's terse poems.

Porter had talked about art after his posing sessions. One afternoon Porter said, "I like your gestural style, it's so expressionistic."

Elaine had asked, "Do you mean like the German Expressionists?"

"No," Porter said. "It's much more like the abstract painters down here in the Village. Like Bill or maybe sometimes like Gorky."

"Yes, I suppose you're right," Elaine admitted.

"If you compare your art to poetry, it would be like Ginsberg's."

"To me," Elaine said, "a painting is primarily a verb, not a noun. A painting is an event first and only after an image."

"That's a very eloquent way to express it," said Porter. He wrote down her remark and later she read it, only slightly revised, in an art journal.

While she laid out her tubes of paint, brushes and rags to wipe the brushes clean, she thought about last night's fight with Bill.

Drunk again, he had lashed out at one of her portraits. Which one had it been? Elaine couldn't remember. She drank too much herself, feeling the cheap wine swimming in her bloodstream. But she didn't say, "Maybe we spend too much money on wine."

Bill had pointed a brush at a portrait. "Why the hell don't you paint a total abstraction? Why are you always connected to the figure or some boring still life?"

"What are you saying?" Elaine turned around, took a large swig from the mason jar she used as a glass. "Your own pictures show all those fat woman with the horrible teeth, leering like hyenas."

"They aren't fat!" Bill slammed his fist on the plank table.

"They are too," Elaine spat back. "Buxom, that's the word for them."

"Okay, buxom. Maybe a well-built woman would be better than a skinny bitch like you." Bill laughed.

"You should know. You sleep with your models."

"Well, you sleep with our friends, and that's even worse," he shouted. "How about Harold Rosenberg?"

"That was just so he'd write good reviews of your stuff, so you'd get a decent gallery." Sleeping with Harold wasn't simply about promoting

27

Bill's career, Elaine thought, as she squinted into her empty glass, wishing it was full. But Bill didn't have to know everything, and anyway, he slept around much more. She lit another cigarette, even though the doctor said she smoked too much.

"Let's not argue about who we sleep with outside of this apartment. What the Hell difference does it make?" Bill gave her his smile that could melt an ice mountain.

"You're right. We don't care. It's 1951, and we can do what we want. There's nothing so boring as middle-class values."

She felt exhausted and stretched out on the cat-shredded sofa.

Elaine had been friends with Lee Krasner, Pollock's wife, for a few years. She thought herself a better artist than Lee, but at least when Lee visited, she had another woman to talk to. Lee breezed into the apartment, her slacks slightly paint-stained, though not as badly as her shoes. With her hair cut short and the navy blue pea jacket, she looked sort of like a sailor. Elaine smiled at Lee and closed the door.

Lee asked, "What are you grinning at? Me?"

"Oh no," Elaine lied. "I've just been looking at my last Bacchus painting and I think this time maybe I got it right. Come over here and look at it. What do you think?"

"Okay, put me on the spot before you even offer me a cup of coffee, Elaine. But yes, it's more abstract than most of your portraits. I like it better the more I look at it."

"I'll paint a series of them," Elaine said. She liked the blues and greens, laid on in great swatches of thick paint.

"Well, we are revolutionary. Someday people will look at our work and understand what abstraction is all about, that's it's the process of painting," said Lee.

Lee is so full of bullshit…she loves to pontificate, thought Elaine. "Yes, we deserve to be in museums and become old fossils, right?" She put a cup of coffee in Lee's hand, but noticed that Lee left the cup on a table and then walked around the room.

Lee stopped ever so briefly in front of the portraits, but seemed more concerned with some canvases by Bill, which lay stacked in a corner of the apartment.

"Bill's onto something important," Lee cooed.

Nice the way you came over to look at my new stuff, Elaine wanted to say aloud, with a sarcastic knife's edge. But she kept mum, not saying anything.

Lee smiled. "Wasn't the show Sidney Janis just gave all of us a great one?"

"First I thought so," Elaine replied. "But he called it 'Artists: Man and Wife.' Wasn't that a put-down of the women in our show—you, me, Barbara and Sophie. That sounds like we're just wives attached to men, who are the real artists."

Lee sat down on the thread-bare sofa. "I never thought of it that way. I know we live with men who think that women can't really paint, but I hoped the show would prove we don't just paint crap."

Quiet, Elaine sipped her coffee. Maybe if Lee stopped imitating Pollock's style, she could paint something original. Elaine thought, Women have talent, and we'll succeed just as much as the men, given time.

The next day Merce would return, and the portrait would continue taking shape. She knew she had to be careful, not to mess up what could be a good picture.

Years later, Elaine thought about how so much had changed in her life. It was a Spring afternoon as she waited for her dealer to come over and view her latest works for her next show. She knew that Sidney Janis would either shrug in distaste or else love her latest paintings. He had been supportive for over thirty-five years, and now she wanted him to show her series of bull paintings, inspired by the Paleolithic cave images she'd seen in Spain. Her visit to Spain and the cave in the Pyrennes proved art revolved in cycles: from the cave pictures to 1987, painting had returned to the simple and profound.

The doorbell rang and she left her studio to let Janis in. He shook the rain off his fedora, draped his Burberry coat on the coat rack, and nodded to Elaine. If nothing else, Sid Janis always looked like a god-damned businessman.

"Come see the bull paintings in the studio, Sid." She led the way across the small living room, turning on lights as they went. An electric bulb on a stand, shielded in its aluminum cone like a cocoon, lit up the bull paintings in the studio.

Janis marched around the room, a martinet on parade. But Elaine knew he would quickly make up his mind—he always did.

"Yes, I like them," Janis said. "They're almost as good as your basketball players. That was an even better idea."

Elaine nodded. It was best to agree with gallery owners; they always thought they had to be right. At least her art was now appreciated by a dealer and more importantly by buyers. It had taken years, but in the end, the struggle had ended with success. Tired, she sat down in one of the two chairs in the studio.

She heard Sid talk on, but didn't pay attention to the words. Instead she pictured Bill in her mind: his now overwhelming forgetfulness, the shock of white hair that still flew off his face, his rubber-band wide smile and the surprising softness of his fingers when he rubbed her back. In the past ten years, Alzheimer's had robbed him of so much vitality. She thought of his old concern and affection for her. For that was all that existed by this time: their art and their love.

R. Daniel Evans was a founding co-editor of Philadelphia's *Painted Bride Quarterly*. He has been published in several magazines, including *Cleaver, Jonathan, Art/Mag, Of Leather and Lace, Periwinkle* and *Pangolin Papers,* which printed three of his stories and nominated one for a Pushcart Prize. His most recent publication was in *Courtship of the Winds*.

Robert John Miller

Jars

The pickles were stuck.

Grandpa had ordered the jar opener from the TV, three payments, $19.95. Plus shipping. Plus handling.

They didn't know he'd be gone before the first payment came due.

His 1997 Chevy pick-up, half rusted, sat in the driveway, fully loaded. Mostly canned goods. Some jars. The jars were his problem.

$19.95. Three payments. Plus shipping. Plus handling.

But the pickles were stuck.

His old paper hands could turn a can opener, but nothing in a jar. That was Grandma's job. That, and the pickling. Now he just store bought. That's why the seals were too tight, he thought. That's how we got here in the first place. Too many years, too tightly sealed, dotted all across the country.

Robert John Miller's work has appeared in *New Flash Fiction Review, Peregrine, Monkeybicycle* and others. You can find more stories at robertjohnmiller.com. He lives in Chicago and is working on a novel.

Josef Krebs

Advancing Into the Past

Advancing into the past

I last longer than I last lasted

Treading slowly on unfirm footage

Despite the light

Shining darkness on all who wait

In the early hours

The thoughts that emerge irreligious

Unwelcome but obviously belonging despite

Or to spite

As the jungle moves closer

The air thicker

The dust settling

Eyes wide

The room moving

Sounds unsettling

Noises interpreted to suit the mood

As the clambake comes to a close

On some forgotten beach

Where all is well with the world

But far far away

And a long time gone

Josef Krebs has a chapbook published by *Etched Press* and his poetry also appears in the *Bicycle Review, Burningword Literary Journal, Calliope, The Cape Rock, The Chaffey Review, Inscape, Mouse Tales Press, Organs of Vision and Speech, Tacenda, Agenda, The Corner Club Press, Crack the Spine, The FictionWeek Literary Review, the Aurorean, Carcinogenic Poetry, The Bangalore Review, 521magazine, Former People, The Bohemian, Grey Sparrow Journal, IthacaLit, New Plains Review, Inwood Indiana Press,* and *The Cats Meow*. A short story has been published in *blazeVOX*. He's written three novels and five screenplays. His film was successfully screened at Santa Cruz and Short Film Corner of Cannes film festivals.

Kathleen Latham

Man With a Hoe

We argue in an art museum while lesbians in bad suits and hipsters who take themselves too seriously nod at the exhibits around us. They murmur appreciatively, and I feel duped because I don't get it. Like I've been left out of a joke.

"Tim," my girlfriend says between clenched teeth, "can you at least pretend to try?"

We're standing in the middle of a white-washed room staring at a blob of brown papier-mâché in the shape of a giant turd. As usual, I'm not exactly sure what she's referring to—the turd or our relationship. "I am trying," I shoot back, which is true either way.

She turns and looks at me with a single raised eyebrow. Four weeks' worth of conflict in the flick of a muscle.

"What?" I say. "You don't think I'm trying?"

She sighs—one of her heavy, laden sighs—then turns and heads for the next room. I leave the turd behind and follow sullenly. We pass a light bulb on a block of wood. A mesh basket filled with jock straps. A reading lamp wearing a wig and slippers.

The day is not going like I planned.

We come to a stop beside three Asian girls wearing Hello Kitty backpacks and skull-embossed stockings. They're studying something that looks suspiciously like cat vomit on a fake putting green. None of them speak, but they seem impressed. I am obviously missing the point.

"I thought you liked art," my girlfriend says.

"Art involves paint."

She does the one eyebrow thing again. "Is this about San Francisco? Because I thought we agreed to let that go."

"This has nothing to do with that," I say, which is probably a lie. "This is about being pretentious."

"Pretentious. Really."

The Asian girls side-step away like nervous cattle sensing a storm.

I point at the title of the cat vomit piece printed neatly in the center of a plain, white card: *Nadir*. I try to raise one eyebrow.

"What?"

"You don't think that's pretentious?"

"It's meant to be contextual."

"Contextual? As in, his cat threw up on his putting green? Then call it that. Call it *Cat Vomit on the Back Nine*."

"That doesn't even— "

"Calling it *Nadir* is pretentious. Everything in here is pretentious." I wave my arms a bit too belligerently. "It's all just stuff pretending to be something it's not."

"That's what art does."

"No," I stammer, "no, not always. What about portraits? Or a still life? What about the hundreds of years where artists didn't try to make their work more interesting by giving it titles. They let the art speak for itself: *Girl with Red Hat. Man with a Hoe*—"

"Well, technically those are descriptors— "

"If *Man with a Hoe* was called *Exploitation of the Masses* would that make it better art?"

"Tim— "

"What if it was called *Disillusionment?*"

"Tim— "

"*Exhaustion? Everyman?*"

My girlfriend shakes her head in that annoying way she has, like she understands something I don't. An elderly man in a fly-fishing hat shuffles between us, oblivious to our argument. "You're being ridiculous," she says over his head.

The old man smiles at her stupidly. For a moment, I'm distracted by his hat. Who wears a fly-fishing hat to an art museum?

"Besides," she continues, oblivious to the minnow-shaped lure swimming beneath her nose, "it's conceptual. You see that, right? The idea matters more than the execution."

I open my mouth to reply, but I've already lost the thread of the argument. The fly-fishing hat has derailed me.

My girlfriend pats me on the arm. "Let's just agree to disagree," she says. She's been doing this a lot since San Francisco. Patting me on the arm. Agreeing to disagree. It bugs the shit out of me, because I know it's code for, *I don't want to talk about this anymore.* Still, she takes my hand and gives it what I'm sure is meant to be an affectionate squeeze.

We leave the cat vomit behind and follow the crowd through the next room past a series of canvases each adorned with a single geometric shape. Blue triangle. Orange circle. Yellow square. We stand and study them obediently.

"Don't say it," she whispers.

"Don't say what?"

"That you could have painted these."

"I *could* have painted these."

A gray-haired docent in the corner smirks up at the ceiling as if she's part of the conversation.

"A three-year-old could have painted these," I say louder.

The docent ignores me. Everyone ignores me. They all stare at the shapes as though it never occurred to them to paint a triangle blue, a circle orange. Behind us, two middle-aged men in skinny jeans and high tops murmur something about their perceptual givens being

36

challenged.

Lambs! I want to yell. *Lemmings!* But then I can't think of any more mindless follower types, so I shuffle along with everyone else.

"I still think we should have gone to The Getty," I say for the tenth time that day.

"Of course, you do."

I'm about to ask what's wrong with The Getty, but just then we pass the docent, who nods in our direction and says something that sounds like "Now she choose" or "No issues," neither of which makes any sense, but it makes my girlfriend snort.

"What?" I ask, but she's already pulled open a side door marked *MIXED MEDIA INSTALLATION* and disappeared into the next room. A brief bubble of sound swells out behind her, then the door sucks shut, and I'm left alone with the preschool shapes, the judgy docent, and the lemmings. After a brief hesitation, I yank the door open and follow.

It is dark in the new room. And way too warm. A movie plays on a rotating, double-sided screen. A shadowy figure in a hood is yelling in a deep baritone at a shirtless man. "SAY YOU LOVE ME!"

The camera zooms in on the shirtless man's armpit. He whimpers. The screen rotates. The camera locks on the mouth of the hood. "SAY YOU LOVE ME!" the lips command again, but this time it's a different voice. Female and flirtatious.

That's it. That's all that's in the room. The rotating screen. The whimpering man. The voice from the hood, which is different every time. Old woman. Little boy. Teenage girl. The volume is on full blast.

"SAY YOU LOVE ME!" cackles a witch.

"SAY YOU LOVE ME!" drones a robot.

My girlfriend watches this for a long time. Long enough that I feel like she's trying to tell me something.

On screen, the bare-chested man cowers and whimpers. After a while, his pathetic mews burrow their way into my head, nestling there with unwanted thoughts of San Francisco and unanswered calls and my girlfriend's bare skin on someone else's sheets. A bead of sweat slides down my back.

"SAY YOU LOVE ME!" rasps a really bad Liam Neeson.

I've had enough. I cross the room to a second exit. On my way out, I pass a security guard leaning against the wall. He gives me a sympathetic shrug as if we're compadres—both of us beleaguered and weaponless. The reflection of the film flickers on the sheen of his face like a strobe light. I give him a nod back, and as I pass, I notice he is wearing earplugs.

It is only after the door closes behind me and I am alone in the hallway that this registers.

Earplugs. To block out the sound.

I actually hold my breath for a second, certain that I have stumbled upon something significant. Earplugs. Art museum. That horrible whimpering. I begin to pace—chasing the link, fleshing it out—because suddenly it feels very, very important that I get this right. That I figure out a way to articulate what I'm thinking. So I pace and I ponder, until I've got it, until I'm ready, until my girlfriend emerges and I offer it to her: a small, slim point of connection.

She has no idea what I'm talking about.

"He was wearing earplugs," I repeat, louder than necessary because it's the first time all day I feel like I've gotten something right. "The security guard. Like he has to *protect* himself from the art he's *protecting*. I mean, we're all paying to hear what's in that room, and he's getting paid to not hear it. That's saying something, right? Like, art kills. Or, the joke's on us. The emperor has no clothes. It's ironic, right?" I bounce up and down on my heels, waiting to see what she says. For her face to light up. For her to find me brilliant.

She chews her lip for a few seconds before she says, "Earplugs or earbuds?"

I stop bouncing. "What?"

"Plugs or buds?"

"What difference— "

"If it was an earbud, it was probably like a headset or something, so he could talk to the other security guards."

"He's not guarding the damn President!"

She shrugs, then digs in her purse and pulls out a museum map. "Let's eat."

"Wait, what?"

She flips the map over. Traces a path with her finger. "I'm starving," she says, heading for the stairs.

"Hang on," I say, though I know she won't turn around. I consider staying where I am and forcing the issue, but she's already halfway down the grand staircase. I follow, deflated.

My sneakers squeak on the marble steps, an incongruous sound that makes me think of basketball and last second changes in direction. I wonder for a minute how it came to this. How it is that I always seem to be one step behind.

Up ahead, my girlfriend hesitates beside a dresser without drawers, a pile of candy wrappers, and a creepy-ass puppet all tucked in an alcove. I pass her without slowing.

We eat in the atrium café where chatter from the other tables echoes off the courtyard walls and artsy phrases break over us like the jarring screech of birds: *Cacophony of confluence! Vaudeville of violence!*

I try. I really do.

I sip my overpriced iced tea and listen to her make the old Execution-Is-What-Makes-It-Art argument, and I force myself to consider all the artists struggling in their basement studios. The ones laboring over papier-mâché feces or squares of paint chips glued to a chair or bleeding road signs—taking themselves seriously, because they are serious—expecting to be understood and noticed and appreciated.

Expecting to be exalted. For that chair to go on that pedestal. For that road sign to gets its own white room and bare floor, its spotlight and a line of visitors. Who decides? I wonder. Yes, to the giant turd. No, to the simulated wasp nest with hairbrushes sticking out of it. Who says, this is good, this is crap? If art is in the eye of the beholder, how do you escape subjectivity?

I say all this, of course. Which is obviously a mistake. I pick at my arugula salad topped with gorgonzola and candied pears and say it all as if I'm contributing. As if I fail to notice that I am guilty of the very thing I am criticizing. I see the irony, but I can't stop. It is, I realize, very much like the endless reflections in the mirror-on-mirror piece we saw earlier in the day, the only exhibit I actually liked besides the security guard. Art is a perpetual argument, and I don't know the rules.

I conclude with this statement. Another pearl of wisdom offered up for my girlfriend's approval.

She looks away across the museum courtyard, her eyes shielded by sunglasses, and manages an unreadable nod. I can't tell if she's impressed by my tirade or merely bored.

I'm about to bring up the security guard again—how I still think he's secretly part of the exhibit and why that makes more sense to me than a dresser with no drawers or a basket full of jock straps—when she says, "I wish you'd let San Francisco go."

There's a long silence after this.

I know she's waiting for me to say something, but the truth is, I don't want to talk about San Francisco. Or letting go. I don't want to talk about what's happening at all. So instead I say, "Why did she say, '*Now she choose?*'"

My girlfriend frowns, two tiny perpendicular lines of confusion appearing over the bridge of her nose. "Who?"

"The docent. In the room with the preschool shapes. As we walked by, it sounded like she said, 'Now she choose.'"

She stares at me for a few seconds while she processes this, those tiny puckered lines deepening, then she throws her head back suddenly and laughs.

The laughter surprises me. It rises above our heads like coins thrown to the sky, bright and full of promise. An older couple with a stack of art books between them frowns at us from the next table.

"Your shoes," my girlfriend laughs.

I want to laugh with her, but I am back where I started. In the room with the lesbians and hipsters. My fork is suddenly heavy in my hand. I want to put it down and touch her. Reach across the table, brush her lips with my thumb, and make her stop. But she is still laughing.

"Noisy shoes," she says.

I stare at her blankly, which makes her laugh harder.

"Your shoes squeak," she manages.

And just like that, I understand the conversation is over.

It doesn't matter that I have more to say. That I was about to tell her that if something looks like a pile of trash or a giant turd, maybe that's all it is. That I don't really buy the argument that just because someone bothered to make it, it's art, any more than I buy the idea that labeling something makes it true. Or good. Or worth preserving.

We should know.

But she is still laughing and the snobs at the next table are still glaring, so I smile, as if I'm in on the joke.

I imagine what we look like. A man in squeaky shoes. A woman with hidden eyes, laughing. I am suddenly exhausted.

Nadir, I think, naming the scene. *Disillusionment.*

Kathleen Latham is a native Californian who's been living in Boston long enough to have an identity complex. Her work has most recently appeared in *Hedge Apple, Flash Fiction Magazine, The London Reader,* and *Picaroon Poetry.* She'd like to think there'd be more, but she's easily distracted by computer solitaire and her cat.

Iris N. Schwartz

Words With You

My sentences scamper in, attach themselves to your hat.

"Wait."

You spin around. "Return my thoughts," I want to say, as they're dark characters now, written on your jacket back.

Away from me, will my nouns become nonentities?

Shall I tremble, reading aloud from my third collection of tales? (I've yet to write the second.)

Might my books bellow "best sellers" — only after I die?

You stroll away; manuscript ribbons celebrate my literary demise, trail you like toilet tissue on soles of boots.

Iris N. Schwartz's fiction has been published in dozens of journals and anthologies, including *Anti-Heroin Chic, Blink-Ink, Connotation Press, Gravel, Jellyfish Review,* and *Spelk.* Her short-short story collection, *My Secret Life with Chris Noth,* was nominated for two Pushcart Prizes. Shame, which contains the Best Microfiction 2018-nominated story "Dogs," is her latest collection.

Justin Karcher

Kids Who Die

There's still daylight, but it's raining death in Central Florida

& there are these old white men standing

On the front steps of schools

Holding gold-encrusted bedpans above their heads

& catching pubescent blood

Blowing in the semi-automatic wind.

Then they make speeches high up

In cities upon a hill

Where they drag God out of His grave

With republican voodoo & misspelled tweets.

Everybody's praying, but prayer is like an obituary of birds

Building nests in burning beds.

Let them fly, let your children roam free,

& hope that your skin doesn't burn off.

Anyway, it's probably night time now

& outside our windows, an artillery of smooth-talking carnivores

Stomp through our neighborhoods

Telling everyone to kill themselves.

They're cooking AR-15s on backyard grills

& we're all breathing in the smoke,

Coughing up lungs that we feed to our children.

For the powers that be, extinction can't come soon enough.

Meanwhile, me & my friends are building sleepless ladders

Out of vigil wax & smartphone guts, building something so high

That we can climb to the moon & wipe the shit-eating grin

Off its blood-covered face, because it's nice to have something

That doesn't remind us of dying & afterwards we'll gather

Whatever stars still shining, whatever satellites still singing,

& leave them on innocent pillows like hotel chocolates

& hope that when all the boys & girls wake up,

They'll experience a little bit of sweetness

Before their America begins all over again.

Justin Karcher is a Pushcart-nominated poet and playwright born and raised in Buffalo, New York. He is the author of several books, including *Tailgating at the Gates of Hell* (Ghost City Press, 2015). He is also the editor of *Ghost City Review* and co-editor of the anthology *My Next Heart: New Buffalo Poetry* (BlazeVOX [books], 2017). He tweets @Justin_Karcher.

Tony Burnett

West of Marathon

Marathon has its standards. You're born, school, graduation. You marry, up if you're lucky, but that's where statistics come into play. Sometimes up is down and down is up. You stay on your side of the tracks.

The tracks groan and thunder with trains that don't stop, cargo of many kinds, toxic and benign, even the daily passenger train. The heads of people in some mundane act of relocation rock in unison to the slow rhythm of the steel. The parallel bands of iron circle the high desert like engagement ring and wedding band, eventually leaving the state for points west. An option, Jilly thinks, should she need to disappear. Hopefully, the tipping point will favor her and she'll escape in her personal iron chariot, a 2006 Toyota hatchback, high in miles but tenderly serviced by Junior. If only he treated her as well.

Jilly is familiar with the terminal jolt of endings; high school, barrel racing, wild days, her mother. All things end, bystander beware. Now it's on her to choose. And Nicky, he must be a factor in the choice. What's on her plate? *Scraps,* she thinks. *Scraps are all I have.*

Except the chest, the glowing red Cedar with thick latigo bands. Presently a coffee table, it's been storage, footstool, nightstand, a myriad of uses. She received it from her mother, though by its rustic lines and the pronounced grain of the wood she suspects it to have been selected by her father. Mom's coming-of-age award just before she passed away, it's now empty. She will try to fill the hollow space with what reminds her of home.

It's at least 5° hotter in the restaurant. Jake makes his way to his table in the back near the window. By the time he's seated the waitress is waiting with a menu in hand. Four years, six days a week, and he still doesn't remember her name. She has a pained scowl, a sense that she's paying penitence for something by walking on coals. He asks for migas, even though they're not on the menu. She almost smiles as if he punched a hole in the deep blue funk of her non-air-conditioned life. "We can do that," she says. "To drink?"

"Coffee."

Leroy enters, ducking down to clear the doorframe. "Eggs over medium, bacon and sausage," he hollers at the waitress from across the room. She already knew, four years, the same order every day. He has a 9 mm teak-handled snake charmer tucked in his belt. Jake finally realized his friend was an activist when Texas passed open carry.

"Ain't no snakes in here, Leroy." Jake refuses to let it die. "You're going to shoot yourself in the ass one day."

Jake sips his coffee and ogles his smart phone. He follows his daughter's Facebook posts closer than he does Reverend Gibbons' Sunday sermons. Now she's called him from El Paso, finally needing his help, and the stock trailer's full of cow shit. He can't fathom how social media let him down.

"I always liked Junior," Jake says. "He seemed to take the edge off her, help her grow up a little. I worried back in the day, couldn't get a handle on her."

"My Laurie dated him in high school," Leroy says. "She ended up hiding from his skinny ass. I had to set him straight." Leroy's two fingers tap his belt next to the pistol.

"They were kids then." The migas come covered in pico de gallo and jalapenos just like he ordered, accompanied by a small plastic cup of innocuous looking salsa. He dumps it on top, smearing it over the pile. "I reckon it'll take a couple of days. First I'll need to hose out the stock trailer. Apparently she put her stuff in storage. Junior said all she left in the house was some furniture and his guitar."

"Where's he been? I thought he was working the Buckland ranch."

"Yep."

"Seems he'd a been home nights. It's only 50 miles."

"I don't know." Jake picks up the phone and scrolls. "All I know is Jilly's gone off half-cocked. Now I've got to clean up her shit. Like the old days."

"You gonna bring her back?" Leroy asks.

"I'm going to talk to her."

"You can save a couple of days and just call her for that."

Jake looks at Leroy as though the big man had spoken Swahili. "This is Jilly we're talking about." He shakes his head. "She's got her mama's mule-brained stubbornness."

"So what are you doing here?"

The aggressive beauty of the first bite of migas lights him up like the Fourth of July. He rips a paper towel from the depleted roll in the center of the table, wipes his eyes and blows his nose, making sure the waitress doesn't notice.

Leroy cuts his over medium eggs in the shape of a tic-tac-toe with his butter knife, expecting Jake's standard line. Four years, six mornings a week. Usually it still elicits a humorous taunt. *"Leroy, don't let them eggs get away from you now. Better put them in their place."* Today nothing. Jake looks out at his well-worn ranch truck hoping he won't have to drive to El Paso, knowing he will. He continues to stare at the phone beside his plate, against cowboy rules, as if he expects it to sprout a red tail and horns.

Jake glances out at the pale cerulean sky then focuses on his buddy who seems to misunderstand the crux of the problem. "What are we supposed to do, Leroy?"

"Let 'em run. Hope they'll be okay. Laurie went through a rough spot, remember? She worked it out."

"I thought Jilly had everything going for her; good, hard-working husband, fine son. She even likes cutting hair. Good at it too from what I hear." Jake can't grasp why his daughter would toss it all away. "She called yesterday. Flew the coop. Quit her job. Now she wants me to help her get settled. I reckon I don't have any choice."

Jilly sweeps up the glass, relieved that the shampoo bottle was empty. Adding suds to the mix of shards and water would have been catastrophic in bare feet. The floor relatively clean, she unwraps the towel from her body and spreads it on the tile.

She runs to the front door, sets the deadbolt, then sprints back to the bathroom hoping little Nick slept through the ruckus. *That son of a bitch can sleep with the horses until I'm gone,* her brain still screaming from the near-death experience. Back in the bathroom she kneels on the towel as if in prayer and unscrews the bathtub drain stopper. It'll be showers until I'm somewhere else. I may be made of water but I can't breathe it.

Water. It leaks from hoses connected to pressure washers when seals are worn and brittle. It mixes with cow shit and runs in globules from the open gate of a stock trailer; aromatic, pungent, lashing the high desert air with putrid vapor. It clings to broken glass on tile floors in rural love nests gone rancid, once a sanctuary now a hovel. It closes lungs, blinds eyes, and dampens sound. It chills skin and membranes and thoughts and reasons.

Since the water, the hands on the shoulders, then the throat, the terror in her chest. Since the door slamming, the pink clumps of his skin under her nails. History. This. This thing. It will never happen again.

"Daddy gone?" Nick toddles to the front door almost reaching the knob. Jilly picks him up, cuddles him in her terry cloth bathrobe. "Yes, honey. Daddy's gone."

Jilly waited, three weeks and two days. Finally Junior packed for roundup. Jilly packed too. It wasn't difficult to find a job in El Paso. It wasn't even difficult to avoid telling her coworkers at Hair Raising Salon when she'd be gone. She actually relished the dramatic role pretending Junior's assault was no big deal. The night before she left she gave him the ride of his life. He lasted more than eight seconds, barely, but that made him the winner.

Jake is another story. Once upon a time Jake Steagall was a pillar of the community; tall, broad shouldered, centered, a man of casual and competent control. Then came Jillian. Jake's lanky and compassionate motions became the star Jilly orbited around, an elliptical asteroid smashing orbit, almost too reckless to prevent her darting off into the ozone. Jake tried, he really did, but finally he relinquished her to her mother, a similar planetary object who'd found her way into his cosmos. Jake never recovered. He felt the eyes of his little town judging him harshly for his inability to train-up his unruly daughter.

The dog days heat sizzles the concrete, humidified by the puddled stench of soggy cow dung, the stock trailer now clean enough to haul human belongings. Six phone calls, maybe eight, all unanswered, just a text reply with an address. He couldn't stall any longer. Everything she has in storage only fills half the space in the 16 foot trailer. Reluctantly, Jake pulls onto the highway. Seems like every time he leaves the ranch these days he ends up driving into the sun.

Jake parks behind a warehouse, the stock trailer rattles with every pothole. Across the parking lot are faded lime green doors, He finds the one with a peeling gold 18 on it and pounds it with his fist. The door swings wide and a chunky blonde smiles up at him. "Hi Daddy. How was the trip."

Jake charges in. "What the hell, Jilly? What's got into you." Nick waddles in from the bathroom dragging a trail of toilet paper.

"Peepaw!" Dropping the paper he wraps around Jake's boot. "Hey Buddy! Has your mom lost her marbles?"

Jilly picks up Nick. "Let me finish changing him. There's beer in the fridge. Grab one, get me one too."

"It's 4:30 in the afternoon."

"You're staying over right? It's my day off. Lighten up."

"Not until you tell me what the hell's going on."

Jilly disappears with Nick. Jake looks around the tiny bare room before reaching for the fridge.

It feels strange to be drinking a beer. Jake rarely drinks. It reminds him too much of his wife, how he'd sit on the porch while she paced and pointed and planned. After two or three bottles she'd wind down and join him in the swing, leaning in to make the final sale on whatever project fueled the day's obsession. Here he sits, this time with his daughter in the same animated pitch. Another beer or two and he'll remind her they still need to unload the trailer.

"It's Jillian now," she says, "and I'm going back to using Steagall. I'm having a lawyer here draw up the papers."

"You know this'll be hard, right? Being a single parent has its drawbacks."

"People do it all the time. You did. I came out okay."

"You were 14 when she died, all but raised, and she did most of that."

Winding down, Jillian pulls out a kitchen chair and straddles it backward. "I'll be fine. Junior wants out anyway. He has other interests."

"I'm sorry."

"Not a problem. I see it as an opportunity. I always wanted to see the world."

Jake snorts. "El Paso?"

"It's not Marathon. It's a start."

Jake takes a long drink from the longneck and looks at the off-white walls, the low ceiling, the single window facing the pocked parking lot. Claustrophobia dances across his shoulders. "What about Nick?"

"What about him?"

"A boy needs a daddy."

"Yeah, well – that's up to Junior. He wants visitation, he needs to say so." Jillian hops up to grab another beer. "Ready for another one?"

"Sure." Nick climbs into Jake's lap and immediately pulls open the pearl inlaid snaps of his breast pockets. "Nothing there, Kid, but I just might have some peppermints in the truck. We can check later okay?"

Nick grins. "Peppermints?"

"If it's okay with your mama."

Jillian hands over the beer. "It's your job to spoil him. Heaven forbid I interfere."

"I thought y'all were doing okay. What happened?"

"Some girl from Comstock happened. I could've dealt with that if he hadn't tried to drown me."

"What the hell? When?"

"About a month ago, in the bathtub. I made up my mind then. It just took a bit to get my ducks in a row."

"Why didn't you tell me?"

"I love you, Daddy, but I didn't see how it would matter. You'd have either told me to work it out or you'd have killed him. I worked it out."

"This ain't working it out."

"It is. I don't want Nick to see a lot of fighting. That's not how it's supposed to be." Jillian walks to the window and pulls back the bed sheet that serves as a temporary curtain. "Back the trailer over here. We can unload."

Twenty minutes later only the cedar trunk is left. The other boxes line the bedroom walls. "Put this in the living room. I'll use it as a coffee table. This rents as a furnished apartment but just barely."

Jake grabs one end strap and motions to his daughter to help. "This damn thing's heavy. What do you got in here?"

"My saddle."

"The one you won in San Antonio?"

"Yep."

"Why carry that around?"

"You never know."

Jake contemplates a minute. "Yeah, I guess you could sell it if you got in a bind."

Jillian frowns. "I'd never sell it. No way!"

Some things you figure out. Some you don't. Sometimes you just sleep on it and hope for the best. The empty trailer rattles behind him as he takes the first bite from the convenience store burrito. He accelerates up the I-10 entrance ramp and heads into the sun.

Tony Burnett served as the board president of the Writers' League of Texas 2013 - 2017. He is now the Managing Editor at *Kallisto Gaia Press*. In addition to publications in over 50 literary journals his books include the story collection, "Southern Gentlemen" and the poetry collection, "The Reckless Hope of Scoundrels".

Kathryn Fitzpatrick

Guano Couch

Joe's got this bat now, lives between the screen and the glass in the barn window, rolled up snug like a body in a sleeping bag. Some days he'll tap the glass and it'll wake up, with its pug-nose and yellow eyes, and it'll start freaking out and flapping around—stuck—and one of the guys will laugh 'cause that bat's a dumb fuck for choosing to live here of all the places. We agree it should go somewhere else, like Brooklyn. Or Europe. Portland, Maine.

We all hang in the barn's loft: me and Dennis and Joe. We play Rummy 500 and drink beer that's too thick and tastes like metal. The barn's got a table with cigarette burns, and couches with cigarette burns, a katana sword somebody lodged in the wall but never took out, broken skateboards duct-taped to the ceiling, piles of crumpled receipts and McDonald's cups. There's a World War II model bomb filled with sand and a hole in the wall you can piss out of and a loveseat that's covered in bat shit.

We won't sit on that loveseat; it stays here, cushions ripped and covered in pellets.

Dennis says we're gonna get rabies from the couch, but Joe shakes his head. He's taking a woodlands class at a community college, and he can tell the difference between a red oak and a red maple or something. He's like, *guano's gotta lotta nutrients in it, probably good stuff too, like Vitamin C, or cancer-fighting agents.*

Dennis is like, *why don't you eat it?*

Six years ago, Joe moved everything up to the loft, stuff from the Goodwill or relatives, or furniture people had sex on then gave away, with too many bad memories we never found out about. One of his buddies showed him how to hoist it all up, the same method he used to lift Joe's mattress onto the roof when we were eleven, using a long, flat board and a rope. When Joe's mom got home that day, the mattress with the Spongebob sheets on top of her house, she didn't call the cops, just asked calm and quiet why he still hangs out with the kid who mixed cat litter in a bowl of ice cream and fed it to him.

A lot more people used to hang in the barn, before the bat came, before the years between college and high school graduation dissolved like snow on a tongue. They moved to new towns and states, or got pregnant and married, or joined mission's trips to Kenya and didn't come back. So it's just us now. The bat. The old red barn with the crumbling foundation.

Bat guano is really good to use as fertilizer, we could sell it. Gather it all up in a big plastic bag and go door-to-door like ladies selling expensive lipstick. Split the profits. But this might be made up since the guano couch is floral fabric and mostly rotting. Fading beige. Wilting petals. Looks like it came out of some dead grandma's house, like her kids just wanted it gone and it ended up here.

Every now and then Joe talks about starting a punk band and moving to the city. He's got a guitar and a weird haircut and a strong brow-bone so he thinks he can swing it. Anyways, he can play *Wonderwall*, and knows all the words to every song off *Nevermind*. And Dennis got a new job at a fancy art cinema, the type of place where people pay fifteen bucks to watch unattractive-in-the-right-way actors do weird things with porcelain dolls or fruit, filmed on an old camera with a shaky hand. He thinks he'll make enough to get an apartment he doesn't have to share with his mom. Says we can visit him when he goes.

And maybe we'll all go; the bat'll hibernate in the winter, bury its head in the earth or collect tons of bugs, or whatever bats do when the cold sets in and there's nothing left but icicles hanging from the trees like mucus. The furniture, the katana sword, the skateboards, the piles and piles of cigarette butts scrubbed clean. And the barn, still and unchanging, will disappear, as swift and sudden as a jar pushed from a table, shattering when it hits the ground.

Kathryn Fitzpatrick studies English at Central Connecticut State University where she also serves as Editor-in-Chief of The Helix Literary Magazine. Her work has been previously featured in *Out Magazine* and *The Flexible Persona*, and anthologized in *Flash Nonfiction Funny*. She was the recipient of the Connecticut Young Writers Trust Award for Prose, and lives in Thomaston, CT.

Meg Granger

Hooked Up / Hooked On

Open eyes before light can light the cracks in the blinds—the blanket lies low in a dip between their bodies. His leg bends around her bedding, squid-like. She's a plank, she thinks. Like others, he'll leave soon. She could lie here, under cover, all morning. And he will, he thinks, until she squirms, does something other than lie there all morning. Her upturned lips, fleeting attraction to his one liner, his chum, the sheen of her scaled chemise of turquois blue: these are all facets reeling him still. His rod, clayed into the crevice of his crotch, wants to lower down slowly, tackle cleanly, so his impression shows beyond this one catch. To bring her home, show her off, mount her, stare. She wants to swim away now—far from her own berth—back into open sea's waters. Thrown back. Tossed. Trilling about. Paced breaths, never deep in the lungs; they drown in this stillness swirled only by the fan's propellers.

She could lie here all morning.

And he will.

But a sudden twitch of her tailbone gives her away. He cranks, his jig turned toward rippling in her sheets. Eyes on eyes, he casts another line, angling his barb, dragging, flipping her onto the surface, his thumb over her lip, partially in her mouth. She writhes and springs about, twists from his hard holding, pleading, longing, until the light's shine leaves her eyes and enters the cracks in the blinds—her comforter shifts, and he stands, asking if she wants breakfast.

Meg Granger received her MFA in Creative Writing at Western New England University. She currently works in marketing and events for *BusinessWest Magazine* and she also teaches Freshmen writing as an Adjunct Professor of English. Her work has appeared in *The Merrimack Review* as well *as Crack the Spine*'s "Routine" Anthology.

Lowell Jaeger

Note to an Earlier Self

For clarity sake, let's run the reel back
to the late afternoon on a graveled farm road
through monotonous miles of corn and soy, corn
and soy, more corn and more soy, while an August
sun sizzled your shoulders and thighs, as you pedaled
across the heartland, alone, the longest year of your life,
waiting for a court date, waiting for papers to sign.

Flat expanses of nowhere rose gradually
after crossing a bridge, wooden and decayed,
remember? In the muck below, a muskrat struggled
with a cable snare, thrashing. Another nearby, slick
with scum, also ensnared, but this one lifeless,
drowned.
        It's like the click of shutter — isn't it? —
the way a simple glance can lodge in the brain,
while so much goes by we let pass as if
behind our eyelids there's no one there.

And there she was, one hand raised head-high,

standing on the front porch of a weathered farmstead.

Truly, she was there, in the flesh, wasn't she? The bib

and skirt of her apron stained crimson. Tomatoes, maybe.

Or blood? You, with only a toehold on the cliffs of what's real,

did you invent this apparition? You waved. You saw blood,

and you kept going, muscling your way blindly forward,

immersed in troubles of your own, travails you now know amounted

to vapors of guilt and ghosts of old apprehensions. Was her hand

uplifted

for sake of shielding her eyes from the sun's lowering horizon?

Or was she beckoning to you, and you ignored her call

Lowell Jaeger (Montana Poet Laureate 2017-2019) is founding editor of *Many Voices Press*, author of seven collections of poems, recipient of fellowships from the *National Endowment for the Arts* and the *Montana Arts Council*, and winner of the *Grolier Poetry Peace Prize*. Most recently Jaeger was awarded the Montana Governor's Humanities Award for his work in promoting thoughtful civic discourse.

Arthur Lindenberg

Finding Elijah
Or the Quest for the Seventh Symbol

The Hindu sadhu with blood soaking through his dohti lunges toward Alan, legs collapsing, falling until he and locks eyes to his. He gives a light tap with his forefinger to Alan's forehead, then falls and Hindu dies. Alan's vision blurs as his brain explodes into searing pain and fear and longing. In the chaos, he sees the six integers. Where is the seventh?

Alan lost this key to complete the equation an hour before—or was it ten hours? When was the instant? The red phone back at REF Inc., the phone that only rang for a national emergency: screamed. Alan answered: his wife, Kathy, terror in her voice: shouts of others, banging, a struggle. They took her? Alan wonders. They took her and young Stan. He shouted back. But silence. Was that yesterday? An hour ago?

Rushing down the fire exit to the eerily abandoned lobby of REF Inc., the government think tank where he works, Alan dashed into the street, to be pursued by...were they Soviet agents, or were they ours...that September 13, 1977, morning, the morning was about to discover the symbol that would complete the Equation. Fleeing two miles south along Ocean Way in Venice, California, evading pursuers and more. All he wanted—and wants now is to get home.

Crack...crack...crack...crack...crack...crack-crack...! Twenty feet in front of you the eleven Hare Krishna dance a death dance and fall upon each other, spewing fountains of blood. This violence empties the walkway. Screams fade as the disappearing crowds depart, as the two men in black trench coats, automatic weapons in hand smoking, close in.

Alan looks at the yod in his left hand, given to him by the rabbi who hid him before sending him to the destination engraved on the arm above the gold hand: *Dr. Elijah Abel, Practice Limited to Visionary Psychiatry, 23 Windward Ave., Venice, California.*

One of the men points and raises his weapon. Alan flees down Ocean Way, sprints to corner of Windward Avenue, and turns, looking in the other direction. A naked skateboarder, his body covered in red hair, unkempt red beard swerves toward him.

I'm going to get you, motherfucker!

But on the left stands 23 Windward, in the antique colonnaded building from the 1920s—Venetian style; sign over the door: *Elijah Abel Head Shop.* The instant the skateboarder swoops, and as the men aim their weapons, he dives through the open shop door and closes it behind him.

Inside the shop, Alan Cohen drifts in the silence. Somewhere in his mind, the old Simon & Garfunkel song spins, "Hello darkness, my old friend…"

The only sound is his breathing. Nobody follows him through the door. He looks out of the shop window onto Windward Avenue. No sign of red-haired skateboarder. No men in trench coats. He gazes at a pantomime of strollers, a woman pushing a baby carriage, children kicking a soccer ball, and then moving to the side as a new 1978 Chevy backs out of its parking space and pulls away. Old men, Orthodox Jews, stroll by in black suits, wearing their *kippahs* and the tzitzit from their tallitot visible under their jackets, followed behind by rounded old women with shawls, wearing High Holiday gray dresses. The chatter and movement is mime, as is the lame beggar's appeal approaching them. Teens, in bathing suits, laugh and gesture. Silent laughter paints their lips… a bicycler, his face lost in a bronze beard…blond girl strumming a guitar, and others gathering, throwing coins into a blanket nearby. Shhh…

This head shop has everything but marijuana: Kathy once brought the forbidden weed home. Alan had no idea where she acquired this contraband, but its effects, as he suspected, did not enhance lovemaking, at least not for Alan.

Dim light from above barely let him see the case-by-case collection of the paraphernalia, pipes, hookahs, rolling papers, Buddha statues, walls lined with late-1960s psychedelic posters, the great bands, "end the war," and more.

Alan looks at the engraved yod lying in his sweaty palm. He looks around the store again. Where is the attendant? Where is this Elijah?

Why? Why? Once a colleague told you that the CIA selects unsuspecting experts with security clearances and drugs them to see if they hold up. Is that it? Have they drugged you?

Or was it the Soviets? That explains it. They took Kathy and Stan. No! All is well. This is a big joke! Kathy and Stan are well. This is a drug-induced dream. When he awakens, he will be back in the office at REF Inc., or he will be in your Brentwood home, with a splitting headache. Kathy will still be sleeping.

Yes this must just be an illusion. Soon, the drug will wear off. Perhaps it has started.

Startled by noise from the street, his jaw drops as he sees mayhem outside, a street swimming in blood, death everywhere. The two men, their weapons at the ready, kick over bodies. The naked skateboarder, with an erection that looks like another weapon, points toward the story and yells. Flamenco reaches a crescendo, guitar playing and dancers tapping and screaming.

A click behind him: Alan moves to the back of the store to an elevator that he did not see before. The door opens; he runs inside the sleek silver interior. The door closes behind.

He stops shaking. The aroma of lavender incense soothes him. He stands in the red velvet interior of the elevator, bathed in gentle lighting from an unknown source. He looks at the two buttons side by side on the back: "Up" and "Known." The Up button, well worn and greasy, beckons. His stomach lurches down, and his ears crack as the elevator accelerates upward for minutes then gently stops.

He steps into a barren waiting room. No pictures hang on the monotonous bare walls of this six-foot square space. Two metal folding chairs sit by a table with a small lamp without a shade, holding a dimly lit bulb, the only light. A single closed door sits opposite the elevator. Alan picks up the old copy of *Life*, the only magazine, and reads: "October 11, 1943," two days before date of birth. But how...?

The door opens. The dim light of the waiting-room lamp puts the two figures into silhouette.

So now you know what you have to do. I'll see you for your next appointment. A woman leaving wears a fragrance so familiar, Kathy's favorite. Alan tries to see her face. She rushes to the waiting elevator.

Welcome, Alan. You can come in now. The man beckons, his arms gesturing.

He moves through the door into the bright office. The man with short red hair motions to him to sit in one of two reclining leather chairs, about five feet apart and facing each other. Perhaps he is in his mid-thirties. He wears a black tweed suit and horn-rimmed glasses. Alan has seen him before, but where? Dr. Elijah Abel smiles, an impish smile of the skateboarder, of the surfer, of the elderly rabbi who gave him the yod.

This is your session! Music, one of Alan's favorites, a Bach étude, "The Well-Tempered Clavier", washes over him. The work played exquisitely, to the tempo of a mathematic he studied, yet so unpredictable that when he has turned to the one doubt he has had about certainty of science and math, he has been obsessed with this and other music, carried by it as he is now into the center of the office of Dr. Elijah Abel.

His host sits in the other leather recliner and smiles.

Tranquility: As Alan sinks into the chair, his anxiety and fear vanish. He rises up out of his body and floats up to an empty spot on the top bookshelf, where he sits looking down upon himself and Dr. Elijah Abel, face-to-face in the chairs below.

He studies the posh oak-wood office, a library, with wall-to-ceiling handmade bookshelves on three walls, a curtain covering the fourth. Helter-skelter, books, journals, documents of every size and thickness fill the shelves. Titles jump off the spines of books, classic literature in many languages, going back to Homer; psychiatric journals; religious texts; texts in strange, almost unearthly languages; books of physics and mathematics. On one wall, the books are all the same size, neatly stacked, red covers and spines that are blank: hundreds of volumes.

How can he make sense of this chaos, the antipathy to the calm that he feels? How to make order, but then is order possible if chaos is in charge? Is order but a fantasy that equips us to survive, or to give our survival a purpose?

The clutter descends to Elijah's desk in the far corner of the room. Papers and books flow off the top, covering one or more objects, and spill onto the floor, following a pattern, a stream, seemingly changing as he turns. But on his side of the desk sit two photograph albums.

Stand up and walk around, if you like. Alan goes to the desk. He lifts one of the photograph albums and opens it. On the first page, he stares at a picture of himself, with his parents, Edith and Bernard, and his brother Bill; next to that is a picture of his family together at his high school graduation, and then one of his Berkeley graduation, and finally one with Kathy standing under the huppah at their wedding. Where did

Elijah get these pictures?

Engrossed, he flips the page to see his father's funeral, followed by a picture of his mother's funeral. Like entering through a movie, he and brother Bill exchange blows, wrestle to the ground, shout profanities. He feels the thuds of his sibling's fists smashing his face, some blood trickling, the pain, and numbness... Then Chopin's "Nocturne No. 20": The piano plays from all around him. The notes dance through his mind, one note a mathematical symbol, an equation with the balance hidden—this album?

He turns the pages to other impossible photos and films—this must be a dream—this must be a setup...how can he have pictures of...there is Stan being born, Kathy pushing one last time...there is a red-haired Oliver, Kathy's boss from Cambridge, England—how similar he looks like to Dr. Elijah Abel, the same smile and red hair...the photos: a photo of himself drunk, sitting in a bar next to a woman he has tried to forget—Sheila Martin—Alan with a black eye, cut on the cheek, torn clothes. The anger and remorse: He cannot forget his mother's funeral and the fight there with Bill. He drinks. Sheila stands and he follows, exiting the picture.

And the last photos: Alan picking up the red phone, Alan dashing onto Ocean Way, pursued by the two men in black trench coats. Alan bent over the Torah at the Shul by the Sea, where the rabbi gave him the yod. An angel hovers above him—then the angel points away.

Alan's mouth open, a fear returns until...

Yes, that is your past. Now come.

Elijah takes Alan's elbow and leads him to the curtained wall. The curtain parts and reveals a balcony. They step outside.

Through the colonnade, where Windward Avenue should be three stories down, they hovers over a scene out of one of Kathy's old photographs, taken years before they married, when she was in Varanasi, India. In the cacophony of bells and yells, a wedding procession moves through the narrow, winding streets, beggars and orphans on every corner and every kind of chaos that make this city. The groom wears a ceremonial hat and sits high on a stallion. The bride in a multicolored sari, her hair and face perfectly sculptured, walks alongside, followed by family, friends, musicians playing. In these evening streets, pinwheels flare and spin, and fireworks paint the sky, *crack*. A ripple carries him off the balcony and inside the picture flying and then descending at the Ghats, the steps on River Ganges, the *Blood of Shiva*, Kathy once said. The disharmony of chants and screams from the sixteen temples perched on the Ghats all merge into a deafening atonal madness. Alan walks down the stairs toward the sacred water, inhales the air, putrid with vomit, garbage odors, and burning flesh. On the last step before the water, he removes his shoes and the dhoti. He steps into the river, sewage, lungs, legs floating about. He takes another step, now waist-deep. Praising and preparing for death: This is Varanasi, India, the city of death and of life until death. Other bathers splash and dive under the water. On the steps above, holy men with arms above their heads, but sitting in lotus positions, look ready to bless all who enter.

A bald man adds firewood to a pile beneath two wrapped corpses, a woman and a child. Splashing along the step Alan swims close enough to see Stan and Kathy's faces, about to be immolated by the holy men with torches. A cry!

Say nothing. This is Prophecy.

Elijah's silhouette moves in front of him, cutting off his view. When he passes to his other side, Alan gazes out onto a desolate dry lakebed, at gray sands in dim light retreating into the haze in front of the barren, rugged mountains. The "Ride of the Valkyries" howls like angry wind. Desolate desert. Then swirls of sand-devils dart this way and that way, and wherever they dart, they paint blackness.

The silhouette of Elijah says softly, *this is Destiny*.

Elijah touches Alan's shoulder. Alan closes his eyes. He opens them back in the chair.

A cup of tea finds its way into his hands. He sips the soothing beverage, a mixture of raspberry and mint with a touch of an impossibly delicious alien essence. He calms himself by focusing on mathematical concepts. Alan knows that all truths, all answers lie in mathematics. Kathy and Stan and everyone else: Where are they really? Who am I really? He thinks. Will this be my denouement?

Alan puts the emptied teacup down and searches Elijah's green eyes. He wants to ask how…what?

The psychiatrist answers his unspoken questions about mathematical and scientific certainty, of how the empirical study of a phenomenon allows you to predict what will happen in its future. These are the universal laws of science, sometimes described by and sometimes first identified by the mathematical language that Alan has tried to understand. The big bang, quantum mechanics, relativity, chaos, the dark matter and dark energy that will remain when all is spent, when all stars have flickered out. Not even an atom, or any matter that keeps energy, will survive, at least in this universe.

How does Elijah know? Perhaps he is the prophet. He breathes out and then breathes in. A bond, a link has been created—but it is a contradiction too, a contradiction of chaos… But that is not the only thing: Chaos suggests uncertainty or at least unpredictability within certainty. But how can certainty exist in a human universe of randomness? Nobody knows what goes on inside another human being. Human affairs are beyond the laws of physical science. Mathematics can show trends. That is all.

The universe, Elijah smiles and continues, *the universe has come before and gone before infinite times, and it will come again and go again. I know of your life here and of where you are going.* He goes to the bookshelf opposite Alan, one with blank spines on every shelf. He runs his thumb along one row and down to the next, stops, and takes down a book. He sits next to him and opens the volume. *This is your life. Here, take a glimpse.* He thumbs to a page over halfway in.

Alan looks at an old newspaper photograph of a car crash that took place in the 1920s, the shell of a vehicle he cannot identify consumed in flames. He feels the heat and sees the flames take the writhing bodies about to die, the screams, smell of roasting flesh. Alan is about to vomit when Elijah turns to the next page. Stan, his son, floats by sobbing. Where is he and where is Kathy?

But Elijah turns to the next page: The woman, so familiar, out of a haze, a drunken haze…Sheila Martin—*your wife*—stands next to your son, another Stan, the son of you and your wife… NO. Alan is married to Kathy. Elijah utters, *Stan.* Stan Martin and Sheila Martin. Strauss's "Vienna Waltz" fills the room: one, two, three; one, two, three; love, covered by fear—gut-wrenching fear.

On the next page, he sees his office at REF Inc. There, in the space as large as a lecture hall, stand rows of whiteboards covered with mathematics, numbers, arcs, Greek letters, Hebrew letters, Sanskrit, and alien script, all scrawled in different colors. The keyboard sits on his desk. It is linked to RITA, the world's most massive computer—acres of circuit boards, tubes, reels of tape—underground, under the REF Inc. complex and half of Santa Monica. Music: now a sitar, notes dancing madly in his mind. Alan watches Alan about to input the symbols, to close the equation, to provide the algorithm. Six figures. He closes his eyes, finds the seventh, puts his fingers on the keyboard, and…symbols within symbols, an equal sign and six more…he is about to input the seventh, and…

Elijah closes the book and places the volume back on the bookshelf.

When you were a youth, you rejected the Mathematics of Personal Apocalypse. You had been warned, but you had to see the face of God. Do you remember the algorithm that you inputted into RITA? Ah, but you remember the first six symbols of the equation. The seventh figure could have been...but no, you do not remember the seventh. You forgot the last symbol, as the aleph was forgotten for many years. You still do not know if the Ultimate Theory of Mathematical Limitation exists, not without the seventh symbol.

Elijah Abel breathes out and breathes in.

The truth is that the whole universe has no substance, no certainty. Even time does not exist.

And our time is up. I have other patients waiting. We have made progress. You will find things different, and you will not find anyone chasing you. You must find your answer. Go. Your car is parked where you left it, in front of this building.

What about Kathy and Stan? Alan, for all his brilliance, his two PhDs, still does not understand. He asks.

Kathy is no longer your quest. Elijah escorts Alan toward the door, through a waiting room filled with people laughing, crying, arguing, a couple making love on a sectional sofa. Across the room, a man points a gun with a silencer at the head of a woman. Alan gets into the elevator.

I will see you for your next appointment. The door closes.

Alan rushes out of the shop and into the quiet street. His car: He had parked in the REF Inc. employee lot this morning. Or when was that? How did it get here? His car parked by the expired meter, windshield covered with parking tickets, and his vehicle caked with dust, mud, and soot. Alan wipes the dirt off the windows with his sleeve. He opens the door to his car, puts the key in the ignition. He must get home. The battery sputters and turns the engine over, finally catching. The radio comes on. It is the news: "September 13, 1986. In today's news, Senator Strom Thurmond was admitted to the hospital for tests..."

1986? But it is 1977. What has happened?

Arthur Lindenberg has published fiction in *Edge, Forge, Green Hills Literary Lantern,* and other journals. Currently, Lindenberg is working on a new book-length collection of short fiction. Despite retiring, he continues to teach creative writing.

Eleanor Gallagher

When You Decide to Take Your 2,000-Year-Old God to the Nightclub

Know that the music will seep into the cracks in his big, stone-coated body and vibrate there. The longer he sits in the generous beat, the more unpredictably he will quake, deep in his ancientness, for he will not like to see up close, in sweat and bare skin, the extent to which his dominion has waned.

The scene will trigger in him the energy and conviction with which he crushed goddesses under his thick clay feet so long ago. He will get flashbacks of entire cities smote to ashes by the power of his word; he will remember when he was swollen and damp and powerful. He will not like the contrast of these slithering bodies who give him no thought in the pounding beat.

These bodies, your brothers and sisters, they know there's another god inside who could emerge if you allow the shell of this old deity to shatter. They know how to anchor in what is supple and they would teach you in a heartbeat how to comply with the music inside you, how to pat an old god's crumbling hands like a grandmother, pat him to dust, dance him to the wind. You need only ask.

The last moment to choose will come fast: Trembling, your god will pound his dusty fist on the table and demand to know why you have brought him here. Are the two of you going to destroy this abomination or what? If you let him go on, he will lean in close and hiss that he can see right through your skin that you are one of these and remind you that you deserve to die for being a part of this wickedness.

Now, do it: grab his hand and drag him onto the dance floor, before you believe there is but one path to redemption.

Eleanor Gallagher plays and writes in Tucson, Arizona. Her fiction can be found in Jersey Devil Press, Jellyfish Review, Crack the Spine and Gravel. By day she writes texts and questions for K-12 English tests. In her spare time she serves as Assistant Fiction Editor at Atticus Review.

Martina Reisz Newberry

Winter Damages

You may wonder why I live in winter

when I so love spring and summer. I, too,

wonder that, my friend. Though my paint pot of

gesso is well-used, it never quite hides

the bruises winter inflicts on the days,

trees,

clouds,

grasses,

faces,

souls

and sketches of souls. Winter damages.

and I wish we could be undamaged, not

forever of course, but for a good long

while in which

    all our plants would bloom,

      all our smiles would be returned,

      all our clothes would fit,

      no dust would settle in our rooms,

      no cakes would fall or burn in our ovens.

The truth is that I grow tired of my con-
tusions becoming oblations to a
godhead I fear but don't know how to love.

My spirit wicks three times its size in dread
and regrets during that frigid, gray time,
then converts to clarified butter when

the breezes warm and the clouds embrace white.
I pray for it to be spring then summer
all year. I have no idea what this

might mean to the rest of the planet if
my prayer was granted. What do you think, friend?
Is it an appropriate prayer? If you

love me, you'll say "yes." I'm just asking of
you what I ask of God. Say what you think.
It's appropriate...not too much to ask.

Martina Reisz Newberry's newest collection, *Blues For French Roast With Chicory* is due
out from *Deerbrook Editions* in 2019. Her latest books are: *Never Completely Awake*
(Available from *Deerbrook Editions*) and *Take the Long Way Home* (Available from
Unsolicited Press). Her work has been widely published in the U.S. and abroad. She
lives in Los Angeles with her husband, Brian, a Media Creative.

Tad Bartlett

Boone's Farm from a Sprite Bottle

He slides through the mud, ankle deep, knowing holes can open in this muck where he might sink thigh deep, hip deep, worse. He saw a dog drown here once, a mangy, rib-showing mutt, didn't even whimper as the mud swallowed it up. A few minutes after it was gone, a cat padded light across the surface, its paws like snowshoes. He could've sworn it smiled.

But now, what, thirty years later, that epic bog is just this muddy strip between his old grade-school playground and the pasture lying behind it. A tall chain-link fence encloses three sides of the playground, but this back side has only a falling down cattle fence, rusted barbwire and old oak fenceposts weathered into stone. He knows where to avoid the old dog hole. He remembers the stump where they found the old Playboys stashed. He imagines he sees a corner of yellowed magazine stock sticking out of that stump even now, but knows it's a trick of moonlight or lost love, the remnant of long lost young confusion about the naked body.

He rests his hand on a rusted strand of barbwire. His watch reads 11:38 p.m. His old town is dead, but he is alive. He hoists himself up to balance on the shaky wire. For a second he's heavy, leaden and clumsy, and feels he'll slip in different directions from the wire and topple onto the barbs, or that the rust holding the fence together will give way and he'll drown in the mud like that dog, but then he regains his remnant confidence that he'll never fall, and he straightens up, balancing for just a moment, to prove he can, then hops down to the solid packed playground dirt on the other side.

He walks past the swings and heads to the old playground fort, stout timbers silver in the moonlight. He remembers the weekend in fifth grade when all the parents turned donated railroad ties and used tires into a phantasm of forts and bridges. He remembers later, in high school, sophomore year, sneaking beers and cigarettes up in the fort with friends. By senior year it was vodka and wine and anything cheap or dusty from the back of parents' liquor cabinets.

Even now, under the open night sky, he smells the cigarettes. He hasn't smoked in ten years. He climbs the splintering rungs of the ladder and pulls himself onto the floor of the fort. For a moment, he's face-down to the creosote railroad tie floor, a pain in his back, a cramp in his thigh, his shoulders knotted. The smell of cigarettes is stronger.

"Thought you'd show up here," he hears her say. He looks up, sees her sitting in the opposite corner, graying blonde hair wreathed in the smoke she's just exhaled. He eases himself up into a sitting position, laughs to a joke in his head about how old they both have grown. Twenty-five years since they both left this place.

"Couldn't stand all that back-slapping how-are-ya crap," he says. The wooden walls of the fort feel more closed in, but the sky above had never been more fathomless. "This is the reunion I wanted."

"Reunion with me?"

"Of course not," he lies, hoping she knows it's a lie, "this." He gestures around them with the one arm not killing him from the climb into the fort. "The old playground, this town." A dog barks back in the field, a long way off. "That dog." They both laugh, at their own inside jokes.

He hadn't thought she'd be here, really, but as he drove through the town's deserted streets after leaving the school gym, he'd hoped it, pictured it, pictured her, just like this. He's thinking for only a moment about how they'd made it in this fort one night early in the summer before they left for college, but then he's thinking for many more moments about late-night talking and beers and bottles of bad liquor, generic smokes, holding hands. They'd never been girlfriend-boyfriend, steady dates, lovers, any of that. That one time had just been that one time. Then they left, because that's what you do in a town like that. Like this.

A few hours earlier ...

She sits in her rented car in the lot behind the school gymnasium. The car smells like airport jet exhaust and air freshener and french fries and small farts. She's been in it for almost three hours. Forty-five minutes from the airport in Birmingham, forty-five minutes in the burger drive-in restaurant, slimy jalapenos on the burger, greasy tater tots, and a limeade, not even a diet limeade. She'd wanted it all to taste like then, like it did. High school kids pulled in and out of the drive-in as she sat there, the old lady in the invisible car. They were young and the music pouring out of their car windows sucked. She'd turned up the punk on the rental car's speakers, but it crackled and distorted and Joey Ramone sounded not as menacing as she'd hoped, so she'd turned it back down and rolled up her windows.

Forty-five more minutes of driving around town, past her parents' old house; past her friends' houses, the neighborhoods where they walked down the middle of the street at night barefoot in shorts and tank tops with their hair loosely in braids, drinking Boone's Farm from Sprite bottles, yelling cuss words then diving into azalea bushes to wait until all the dogs stopped barking; past his house, slowly, twice, where the lights were on inside and on the front porch where they used to sit and talk about her boyfriends and his girlfriends and what they would do when they left this place. Then twenty minutes to cross over the river into the next county for the liquor store, twenty minutes back, and the rest of the time sitting toward the back of the lot, waiting and not wanting to go in.

The parking lot is half-full, maybe thirty vehicles, mostly pickup trucks. They have local plates and local red mud splattered on them. Two cars skrit across loose gravel into spots next to each other. Almost identical couples emerge, the men well-weighted around the middle, the women purposeful in their posture. Polo shirts and khaki pants with brown braided belts on the men, linen dresses on the women. Loafers. Heels. Delight and laughter and slaps on the back and kisses on the cheek and cigarette butts thrown to the ground as, with big, certain steps, the four reunited friends walk toward the gym.

She likely knows them, but recognizes none of them. She leans over and digs around in the paper sack sitting on the floor of the passenger side, slides her hands down past the bottle of tequila, the cardboard pack holding the wine coolers. Wine coolers. She was surprised when she saw them in the store. She feels the smooth cellophane wrapper of the cigarette pack, the plastic lighter. She grabs them and steps out of the rental and leans against the door.

She barely recalls what to do with the smokes, all the rituals, and tears off the cellophane before she remembers to pack them first. As she bangs the pack against the back of her arm, he drives into the lot. She knows it's him, though it's a new car, not one she would have ever seen him in before. It has a Georgia tag, Fulton County. He's alone.

She crouches. She feels foolish. She should walk confidently across the lot and greet him, hug him, tell him "It's so good to see you," and he should say, "I've missed you; you're the reason I drove all the way over from Atlanta," and she should say, "And you're why I flew down from Chicago," and they wouldn't be saying this as old or new lovers, but as long lost friends. That's all.

But she doesn't do these things. He gets out of his car, looks around. He's not unrecognizable like the others. He's an older version of himself, but definitely still himself. Sportcoat and khakis, sure, but maybe it's a T-shirt he's wearing under the coat. Without seeing them she knows there are Chucks on his feet. If he knows where to look, he'll see her, but there's nothing else to do but stay crouched. If he sees her now, maybe she can pretend she's only dropped something.

But he doesn't see her. He turns and walks toward the gym. She stands. Four more cars drive into the lot, one right after another. When they get out, they're big men and their wives have big hair, and these are old football players with buzz cuts and cigars and flasks in their pockets and lewd winks for one another.

She gets back in the car. She lights the first cigarette she's pried from the pack, inhales, lets a thin stream of smoke out the open window. She cranks the ignition and drives out of the lot. She heads for the old grade school playground. On her drive around earlier, she'd noticed the field was still behind it, and she bet that the falling down fence was still there, where they would always sneak in on nights like this.

A few more hours earlier ...

When he opens the door to his parents' house, the small entryway seems filled with his mom. "Mama!" he yells out, hoping to make up in volume what he doesn't feel in sincerity or enthusiasm.

His mom puts her hands on his shoulders and leans in to kiss his cheek. "How was your drive?" she asks, but she's already looking behind him, and he knows the next question. "Where's Linda?"

"She couldn't make it, Mama."

She stands back, keeping her hands on his shoulders, appraising him with one eye narrowed. "Is she OK? Not sick, I hope. Unless, you know ..."

Of course she would go to that. "No, Mama. She ain't sick. She's fine. I hear she's fine."

She takes her hands off his shoulders, backs up two steps, enough to put her into the living room. He looks past her, sees there might be a couple new chairs, but otherwise feels like he's eighteen and suffocating again.

"What did you do?" she asks.

"I didn't do nothing, Mom. It's just not working out, is all."

She turns and walks toward the peeling-linoleum kitchen. "Well you just make it work out, son. That's what you do. It's what your dad and I did." She's throwing the words behind her. He ducks, but follows her.

"Too late for that. She's been gone a month. Moved out."

"Well then you get her and bring her back," she says. A blood vessel in her temple is tight against her skin, and it pulsates visibly. A wisp of gray hair has escaped the hairpins of her tight swept-back 'do. She looks years older than the last time he was home. Finally, she turns to him, her face quieted. "Two divorces." It's all she says.

A few more hours earlier …

"Hey, hon'," her husband says, walking down the carpeted hallway to where she's standing by the front door, petting the dog. A collie, large intelligent eyes, immaculately groomed. He could be a show dog, like his parents.

"I'll be gone and back before you know it," she says. "You sure you'll be OK with Jeremy this weekend with all the work you have to do?"

"He's sixteen. He won't even notice anything's different this weekend."

Will you, though? she thinks at him, then says, "I hoped I'd see him before I left."

And then the taxi is honking at the end of the walk. She grabs up her carry-on, pecks her husband on his cheek. The taxi honks again.

Twenty-five years earlier …

His heart is breaking. Two months ago, they'd laid here in the playground fort and held each other, breathing hard, their naked legs intertwined, tucking sweet wine midnight breaths into each other's necks and hair and ears and cheeks. Tomorrow, he'll leave for college in North Carolina, and she'll leave for college in Texas. But now they're sitting, cool, next to each other. Their legs stretch out before them, side by side, touching. Their shoulders momentarily touch when they lean over or breathe deeply or pass the bottle. Each touch strikes him and cracks him.

She has headphones on, listening to the tape he's made her. Not a love mix, but a road-trip mix, a going-off-to-university mix, a best-friends-we'll-see-each-other-at-Thanksgiving mix, a write-me-and-I'll-write-you mix, a send-pictures mix, a let's-call-sometimes-late-at-night-and-tell-each-other-what-has-us-scared mix, a let's-be-happy-for-each-other mix, a hopeful mix, a broken-hearted mix.

Ever since that night two months ago, she hasn't brought it up. Sometimes she looks at him and he knows she's not saying something she's thinking about. But still, there she is, almost every day and night, just like before.

In the daytimes, they hang out under the pavilion at the park by the river, hiding from hot summer sun, listening to someone's boombox, a whole rotating gang, but always the constants are him and her. They all talk or listen quietly or laugh, knowing it's all changing soon.

And at night, they're usually in the car in front of someone's house, or on a dirt road outside the town limits, in the middle of nowhere where the stars press down from the sky. Still always the rotating group, the constant him and her, the loosening tethers.

Sometimes, in the midst of all this, these bodies and friends and words, she looks at him and he looks back until one of them tilts their chin, imperceptible to anyone else.

But tonight, the last night, it's just the two of them in the fort at the grade school playground, where they'd first met in third grade, her first day at a new school.

Her head nods to the music. "I'm glad you put that one on there," she says. "I was just thinking of it when that last one ended, and then there it was." She's smiling, though she's not looking up at him.

He lifts tonight's vodka bottle and takes a swig. It's like shards of glass in his throat, but like saying nothing about that night he plays it off, follows her lead. When he lowers the bottle, she puts a hand on his arm, grips it, turns his arm so she can see his watch.

"Fuck," she says, "it's late." She takes the headphones off. She looks at him. These are the final minutes before they climb down from the fort and walk back, each to their own car. He should say something. He should tell her he loves her.

"I love you," he says, but then cuts back against it, says, "You're the best friend I've got."

Her face starts a smile, then falls blank. "I know," she says, then turns and looks the other way. She draws her legs up close, hugs them. A warm night breeze plays a wisp of hair out of her braid. It tickles his nose. He leans in closer.

She turns back toward him. He's too close. They bump noses, and she laughs, easy. He falls back against the wall of the fort. She puts her hand out on top of his.

"I'll miss this," she says.

Two more months earlier ...

She can't stop smiling. Her whole body is floating and buzzing faintly. She twines her fingers in his hair, his head in her lap.

He moans, a vibration from the back of his throat, out through his hair and into her fingertips. "God," he says.

"I know," she says.

"That was just ..."

"It was," she says.

"Nothing," he reaches for words, "nothing like my first time. I swear," he says. He reaches out and puts his hand on the wine bottle she'd snuck out of her parents' cabinet earlier that night. He holds it up so that it's between him and the moon. "Empty," he says.

"Mm-hm." Then, "That was just your second time?"

"I've told you about that. What a disaster. I had no clue." He puts the wine bottle down heavily.

"You're drunk," she says.

"Probably. But so're you. If I am." He sits up, leans against her. "You tell me all your stuff, too, don't you?"

She closes her eyes to stop the world from spinning. "Of course."

He puts his arm around her shoulders. They don't say anything. She savors it, but wonders how drunk he is, really. They've often ended weekend nights together, a little tipsy, or a lot, sharing a couple triumphs, though usually more failures and confusions. But they've never ended up doing this. She'd wondered, though, and wanted.

"What took us so long to do this?" he asks, and her heart skips.

"Maybe we weren't meant to screw up our friendship?" she asks in return.

"Just friends?" he asks.

"No, no," she says. "Just, we had to get that part right first. Now be quiet. This is where we can mess it up."

And so they sit, his arm around her, her body curled up against his, and the night opens up around them. Cicadas saw in the field behind the playground. A distant dog barks. Far up on the bypass an eighteen-wheeler grinds its gears, blasts its horn. A baby in a house down the street from the school cries in its crib, its wails carried through an open screen window.

She wonders if he's asleep, but then she hears him wet his lips, then he says, "I hope I remember this in the morning. I hope I remember it always."

Tad Bartlett received an MFA in fiction from the Creative Writing Workshop at the University of New Orleans, where he was a reader for *Bayou* magazine. He is now the Managing Editor of the *Peauxdunque Review*. His creative non-fiction has been named a "notable" essay by *Best American Essays*, and has appeared in *The Chautauqua Literary Journal, The Bitter Southerner*, and the online *Oxford American*. His fiction has been published by *The Baltimore Review, Carolina Quarterly, Stockholm Review of Literature, Bird's Thumb*, and others.

Nancy Jorgensen

Muddy Perfection

Adoption, they suggested. Or foster parenting. Both were dirty business. Secrets revealed, privacy relinquished, just to become three. She created a different perfection, cleaning, mopping, scrubbing, dusting. Today, Clayton gifted her a pie, mixed with water, earth and love, patted firm by short chubby fingers. She laughed when it dripped on the floor.

Nancy Jorgensen is a musician and writer. Her 2019 memoir, Go, Gwen, Go: A Family's Journey to Olympic Gold is published by Meyer & Meyer Sport. Her choral music education books are published by Hal Leonard Corporation and Lorenz Corporation. Shorter works appear at Cagibi, Prime Number Magazine, Coffin Bell, the Milwaukee Journal Sentinel and elsewhere.

Anum Sattar

Manipulation

This poisonous vine blames me that I have towered above her,

and made her anchor her tendrils around my leafless boughs,

but in my defense, I merely spread out my arms to shield her

from the menacing birds that snatched the berries off her stalk,

and thus, let her clamber her way onto other shoulders

and in doing so, she leaves me to rot away, until I finally fall.

Anum Sattar is a senior studying English at the College of Wooster in Ohio, USA. Her poems have been published the *American Journal of Poetry* (Margie,) *The Charles Cater: a working anthology, 50 Haikus, Stuck in the Library, Broadkill Review, Poetry Life and Times, Triggerfish Critical Review, Packingtown Review, Blithe Spirit, The Mythic Circle, HOBART, SurVision Magazine, Literary Juice, Coal City Review, Crack the Spine,* (online and print anthology,) *Lowestoft Chronicle, Taj Mahal Review, FIVE 2 ONE: An Art and Literary Journal, The Linnet's Wings, Ragazine, Better than Starbucks! The Florida Review, Grey Sparrow Press, Oddball Magazine, Artifact Nouveau, Off the Coast, Strange POEtry, Between These Shores Literary & Arts Annual, Conceit Magazine, A New Ulster, The Cannon's Mouth, The Journal of Contemporary Anglo-Scandinavian Poetry, Wilderness House Literary Review, Poydras Review, The Cadaverine, Verbalart: A Global Journal Devoted to Poets & Poetry, The Wayne Literary Journal, The Ibis Head Review, Avocet: A Journal of Nature Poems, Poets Bridge, Deltona Howl and Tipton Poetry Journal.* She won the first *Grace Prize in Poetry* and third *Vonna Hicks* Award at the college. Whenever possible, she reads out her work at Brooklyn Poets, Spoonbill and Sugartown Bookstore, Forest Hills Library in New York City and the Cuyahoga Valley Art Center at Cuyahoga Falls, OH. And she was recently interviewed at Radio Free Brooklyn.

Kristen M. Ploetz

Life Without Anesthesia

Outside the picture window, the *Phragmites* undulates. Reed-thin blades arc and sway in the wind. The ballet of lithe hunchbacks nod their taupe-colored tassels in susurrant agreement: another storm is coming.

Once aggressive, now invasive, they are her only reliable informants.

She walks quickly to the whitewashed kitchen and doesn't notice when her heel catches on a loose nail in the floor board. Small circles of blood stamp the rest of her path to the shelf anchored high on the far wall. With the tips of her fingers, she pulls the box down. The sticks inside shift and click in her urgency. There are more than thirty in her collection and she will need a sturdy one today. It's been a long time coming, though it's not the big one yet. She worries that the sticks have been dwindling at a faster clip. They might not hold for the rest of the season.

In the stillness of determination, she is mesmerized by her choices. Yellow birch would show teeth marks. Too soft. Better for the joy of popsicles and flimsy rafts. Better for the first few lies. She's uncertain why it's still in the box. Tiger maple and cherry . . . both pretty and sturdy, like her. The old her. That's why she wishes she had Brazilian walnut, even a short length, because inevitably, she will need something indestructible. She knows it's not a true walnut. It's a misnomer. A fake. Another imposter, just like him.

She chooses the hickory and puts the box away as the key turns in the front door.

With slow movements, he hangs his coat in the closet. Silently, she watches him, now aware of the throbbing in her heel. He pulls something out of his pocket and tucks it into his leather bag on the floor. When he starts toward the kitchen, she slides the stick between her teeth and bites down, ready again to bear the pain of what he's about to tell her, revealing the jagged triangle of space where her tooth chipped the last time.

Kristen M. Ploetz lives in Massachusetts. Her recent short fiction has been published by *Wigleaf, FIVE:2:ONE, jmww, Gravel, Hypertrophic Lit, Lost Balloon, Maudlin House,* and elsewhere. She is currently working on a few projects, including a collection of short stories, and is Creative Nonfiction Editor for *Atlas + Alice.*

Olivia Gunning

Up Your Skirt

By the time you get home, half the school has seen up your skirt. They've seen the emerald green underwear and the soft ridges of cellulite that flock about your thighs. They've seen the strands of pubic hair escaping the edges of your gusset and they've seen the splatter of spots on the underside of your buttocks.

You'd been in the comfortable state of innocence, hailing one of Casablanca's red taxis, rejoicing in the warmth of a summery Friday. You were ready to reach home, take off your clothes and shower away the sticky mix of sweat and diesel.

Your taxi stops to pick up a couple of extra passengers and you feel the buzz of your phone. An email sent from anon@anonymous.com. Subject line: *Up Your Skirt*. You see the screen shot, the phrase "Asking for it" typed across it, the figure "985 views" at the base.

It takes a moment for you to recognise your own body, but you see that it is, undeniably, yours.

You open the message as a new passenger squeezes into the taxi. A thick-fleshed, elderly lady, Berber tattoos on her chin, Her stocky shoulders press against yours. You feel her peering at your phone. Did she see? Did she see that shot of your undercarriage? The shot that has delivered an almost fatal sense of nausea and stony paralysis.

You thought you were safe, sashaying through the classroom, up and down the aisles, confident, cool-headed, sure of your authority, certain of the respect you procured.

You were so very, very wrong.

You'd never had imagined that one of them – and will you ever know who? – would flick his (or her?) phone onto camera mode and stick it between your legs. Think back to all the classes you took that afternoon. How many students called you over for help, made you to stop and bend forward, just a little, just enough, to look at their pages.

You didn't feel a thing.

It can't have taken even an hour to spread over numerous social media networks, slide silently into the screen of every kid at school.

The taxi stops for you to climb out. You have to scramble over the old Berber lady, who doesn't want to move, because the left-hand doors of Casablanca's taxis are always locked. You pull your skirt close to your legs. Is everyone watching? With trembling hands, you punch in the code that opens your building. As the lift takes you to floor five, you pray nobody will get in.

You open the front door to your flat and crumple onto the sofa beneath tears of something that outshines anger and humiliation and rage. Something that trumps them all. Something that you've never felt, even though you believed you'd experiences every shade of anguish.

Your blue skirt, its white lining slightly frayed, rises up mid-thigh as you lie back. You touch that thigh, feeling the mottling skin and the prickles of half-shaved hair.

You hadn't even considered epilation.

Elsa is away this weekend. You're alone. You miss her even though living with a late twenty-something makes you uneasy at times. It seemed a good idea taking a tenant to make ends meet and, you may as well admit it now, fill in the gap created by solitude.

But now you wonder. Those evenings spent being out-drunk by kids fifteen years your junior, weren't you ridiculous? Didn't you notice that your skin reddened as theirs stayed satiny-clear? Was it so difficult to hear the slurring of your voice dribbling on endlessly on outmoded conversation topics?

You shook it off, didn't you.

Easier to ignore the pitying murmurs of Elsa's friends as she explained how you're single at forty-eight. That divorce rapped at your door only 18 months after the wedding vows. That you grew bored of your marriage that fast.

Elsa doesn't even know about your three miscarriages that flowed from the place now immortalised by the fingers of a thousand teens, clicking you, hashtagging you, sharing you. That place which is now the source of guffawing and urgent whispering behind the bedroom doors of innumerable high-schoolers.

Elsa is not here. But you, you are everywhere now.

On your way towards the shower room, you stop, remembering your Friday night ritual, whereby you undress in front of the fridge, take a beer into the shower with you and bask as warm water cleans away all the grot that 150 students have belched, coughed and sweated into the classroom.

But you don't want to do that. You don't want to take off your clothes there because you'll have to walk past the hallway mirror – a full length.

You shower in the half-darkness. You touch the thinning hair that is no longer so naturally blond. You take a fierce mitt and scrub viciously at the drooping skin and you turn up the heat because maybe it will scald the shame out of you.

You wonder about leaving. Why *don't* you go home, back to England, try and start again? Retreat back into your old life from which your friends have departed, bought big houses in picturesque villages with gardens full of dogs and swings, sheds with projects in them and vegetable patches producing plants nobody grew twenty years ago.

Time has, indeed, passed without you.

Who would employ you now? Who wants an English teacher in England who's been away for almost two decades? Your CV is centred elsewhere, your experience is irrelevant.

Besides, you've always liked your job. You're good at it. A beacon on the team. Your lessons are inventive, you're enthusiastic about projects. You've got spark. Students and parents like you. You're nice to everyone and respected by the administration. Even the director made complimentary remarks on your last report.

You picture the director in his office. You imagine contacting him about this incident, to complain, to protest. You envisage explaining the event. Would he ask for evidence? Would he, too, be party to the image of your subcutaneous fat rippling about your ill-fitting underwear? Would you be able to sit opposite him in his office with all that leather and dark wood, recounting it all in plain words?

"Sir, they photographed my private parts and showed the world."

Wouldn't he silently wonder: *Why the hell does she dress like that?*

All of a sudden, you recall the style duo you saw on morning TV years ago. Two women who taught other women how to dress, told them how they were doing it wrong. They distinctly stated that *"no woman over thirty-years-old should ever, ever, wear a mini-skirt"*.

You, pushing 50, thought you were exempt. You considered such views dated, unevolved.

You were wrong.

Climb out of the shower and swaddle yourself in that enormous dressing gown, the full-length one with the hood that you like wearing in winter. You lie on your bed in the foetal position.

It is dusk and the mosques are calling over the city. The seagulls are drifting through the falling layers of sunlight. Car horns are declaring the weekend. You feel solace in the familiarity of these sounds.

You know that with time, routine has brought comfort. That's what you liked about going to work, about having a regular timetable, the familiarity of the same faces at the same desks.

That's what you liked before.

Olivia's fiction has been published in *The Forge Literary Magazine, Hobart, Pithead Chapel,* and *Monday Night Lit,* among others. As a journalist, Olivia has written for *Fodor's Travel Guide, The National, Breathe Magazine, Elle Decoration,* as well as several travel supplements. She left her native London years and years ago to write, teach, and live is Casablanca, Morocco.

Rose Maria Woodson

Confetti

Snug in your job & quarterly reports,

you think you've arrived,

going nowhere fast in Damascus traffic,

idling alone

in the back of a cab, one

pedestrian after another

passing you by when you turn & see…

the couple,

him, deep brown skin, dreads,

her, a caramel latte cameo framed in   cumulus black hair,

leaning in to each other,

over Italian ices,

lemon, maybe, or coconut,

at a small

outside table

leaning in, like private towers of pisa,

slanted towards love, or something close

to it, bigger than life & laptops,

their Olympus clouded in laughter &

you would die to hear the punchline &

you could die waiting for a green

light & you

try to remember the last time you felt breath

leaving you in laughter,

leaving you becoming

confetti.

Rose Maria Woodson holds an MA in Creative Writing from Northwestern University and an MA In Community Development from North Park University. Her chapbook, *Skin Gin*, was the 2017 winner in the *QuillsEdge Press* chapbook contest. Her poems have been published in numerous journals including *Kettle Blue Review, Clarion, Gravel, Wicked Alice, OVS Magazine, Magnolia: A Journal of Women's Socially Engaged Literature, Volume II, Jet Fuel Review, Stirring, Scape Goat Review* and the *Mojave River Review*.

Redfern Jon Barrett

They

Lakshmi laughs like a seagull, daw lips sugared with pink cotton candy.

"Just look at poor Seo-yun, look how terrified fi is!"

"I told you, it's not *fi*, it's *they*." Already Seo-yun is dizzy with vertigo, squinting at the sun-glittered ferris wheel. "Just call me *they*."

"Fi's always been terrified of heights, ever since fi was little." Becca never misses an opportunity to gloat over how long hu's known Seo-yun. The intent isn't lost on Lakshmi: di stares out to sea, sullenly piling fluffy clouds into daw mouth.

"I said don't call me *fi*," Seo-yun insists. "Imagine if we based our pronouns on something else, something other than race. What if we addressed people differently just because of their sexuality, or their religion, or even their gender? How would that sound?"

Becca doesn't respond. Lakshmi picks at daw snack. Nothing passes between the three as they hand over tokens, as they wait. Nothing but the soft smacking of spun sugar and the distant crackle of waves. It's isn't until they're seated that Becca speaks; as they're rising through the air. Seo-yun's palms sweat with fear, clasped firm against the rail.

"So you're really sticking with this *they* thing?" Becca sneers. "Like you're not even Asian, like you're not anything?"

The taunt is twofold: hu holds both hands in the air as Seo-yun's knuckles whiten.

"Oh, leave fin be," Lakshmi intervenes, before correcting dawself. "Leave *them* be."

"I'm just asking a question!" Becca insists, jaw clenched with indignance, hands still held aloft. "Seo-yun's the one saying it's wrong for me to use *hu*, like it makes me some sort of racist. I've used it all my life. It's what I want to be called."

Still the wheel turns, still the car rises: now the whole promenade is visible. An endless parade of graying hotels stare forlornly out to sea. Seo-yun holds firm; tries not to glance down.

"You can use what you like. But I started using *they* and I prefer it."

Becca snorts in derision. Lakshmi is listening. Seo-yun continues.

"Of all things shouldn't we be able to choose what people call us? Isn't that a basic mark of respect? I'm not going to start calling Lakshmi *they*, I'll call daw *di* as long as *di* likes. And Becca, as far as I'm concerned you'll always be the biggest *hu*-bitch I know. This is just for me. Am I really hurting anyone?"

The question hangs; the city spreads below. Seo-yun's grasp tightens as the capsule creaks and rocks, stomach lurching with each sway.

"Whatever. So long as I don't have to use it for myself," Becca declares, hay hands finally lowered. "So fine, you're *they*. Happy now?"

"They're just a big old ray of sunshine," Lakshmi teases, leaning over to wrap an arm around Seo-yun. The sudden shift swings the car—Seo-yun cries out as Lakshmi drops the cotton candy. The three watch the fluffy pink cloud as it's carried away by the breeze, as it glides above the silver sea.

Redfern Jon Barrett is a writer and activist. Author to novels *Forget Yourself* and *The Giddy Death of the Gays & the Strange Demise of Straights,* their stories have appeared or are upcoming in *Booth, The Sun, Passages North,* and *Flash Fiction Online,* while their other writing has featured in *Guernica, PinkNews,* and at the National Museum of Denmark. Redfern has been a finalist for the Bisexual Book Awards and Scotland's HISSAC prize, and longlisted for the Royal Academy/Pin Drop Short Story Award. Their personal life and campaign work has been referenced throughout the press.

Margaret Karmazin

Outside

"Do you ever spend time outdoors?" my well-meaning friend asked, her voice, probably unbeknownst to her, a bit heavy with judgment. She is only one of several people, including my husband, who periodically hint at or question me on this issue. This time, a delivery truck arrived and I had to cut her short, so never answered the question, but I'll do it now.

I spend quite a bit of time looking out the sliding glass doors that open from every downstairs room in our house and while I greatly enjoy what I see out there – lush woods, grass, birds hopping around or chattering as they fly tree to tree, mossy rocks, chipmunks darting madly, flowers and glimpses of sparkling lake between the trees, do I enjoy actually being out there sitting or walking about? Not much.

The moment I step outside, bugs attack. They adore the scent and taste of my skin. While they feed, they use their tiny cellphones to text their friends and these soon arrive from miles away ready to party. Something is always crawling on me somewhere; I spend most of my time outdoors slapping at my body. A horsefly has his thick proboscis drilled into my upper arm, another variety of fly buzzes my nose, a gang of gnats dive-bombs my eyes, mosquitoes just got my ankles, a spider is on my pants and a wasp is circling in a threatening manner. They like my hair too, love to crawl in it and expire in there messily when I murder them. The bugs I actually enjoy, dragonflies, damselflies, butterflies, ladybugs and beetles are nowhere to be seen. Just two minutes outside and already welts are forming that will fester and itch for days, if not weeks.

Anytime I have tried reading outside, I spent more time swatting bugs than absorbing anything on the page, in the process smearing the paper with blood. The pages flip over in the breeze too. As for painting - how did Van Gogh and Monet stand it? Bugs crawl on my canvas and into the paint and at least two die in my water cup, while others perform their usual carnivorous feast on my body. Sweat runs into my eyes and everywhere else. A sudden gust of wind knocks everything over. I have to use the bathroom and it is far away. Any artistic or literary mood quickly vanishes under such an assault. So much nicer to paint inside where the temperature is controlled, nothing other than kitty-cats bother me and I can watch a low key documentary while I work. Or read on a comfortable futon with a cat purring beside me.

Well, judgmental people would say, "Why don't you take walks outside?"

In my past, which has been relatively long considering how ancient I am, I have taken many walks outside. In my youth, this was something I did as a matter of course, walking to school or class. When school was out, we were outside as soon as possible in the morning and stayed until we were forced back inside for meals. When a child, being hot or cold did not bother me, neither did being sweaty. I don't remember bugs driving me as crazy as they do now. We lived in a typical American housing development with a woods behind our street and my friends and I were in those woods playing Sheba - Queen of the Jungle, Indians, or Robin Hood, building tree houses, dangling our hands and feet in a rocky stream or just walking the trail. If we weren't in the woods, we ran in the streets or rode our bikes for hours in the blazing sun. My bother and I hiked the mile and a half to the swimming pool, swam all day and then walked home. There were no scary animals about, just the occasional loose dog, and nothing to hurt us. The outside *belonged* to us.

During college, I took solitary walks, starting in town and walking until out in the country before turning back. We trekked across campus to classes or dorms, strolled to restaurants and everywhere else. No one I knew had a car. And later when married to my first husband and living in a town hear Philadelphia, I walked to the store, rode my bike and roamed the neighborhood days and evenings, enjoying peering at houses and into front picture windows.

Now I live beside a lake in a rural, very wooded area. There are no sidewalks. For years, I have done an hour to hour and a half workout upon arising in the morning, using a rowing machine or combination of aerobic videos and elliptic machine. Once that's done, I bathe or shower, get dressed for the day and enjoy feeling cool and clean and undisturbed while I work. The animal population is active and bears, coyotes and fisher cats visit, and several people have seen cougars though the game commission denies their existence. The bears have become overly familiar in some cases and my husband carries a gun for protection if he in in the woods or mowing a field. Anymore, I would not take off by myself through the woods or even around the lake. I saw a bear in our long driveway. So, what's left for me is to talk down the hill to the lake to sit and be devoured by bugs or to sit on the front deck and be devoured by bugs or to remain cozily inside and do anything I please while enjoyed the beautiful scene right outside the sliding glass doors.

Some people seem to put a higher value on being outside than on being indoors, as if sitting in a lawn chair outside trumps painting a picture, writing a story, or baking a cake inside. A person at the kitchen table paying her bills is inferior to a person drinking a beer in a hammock outside. A man in his garage building bookshelves is second rate, while someone in the driveway washing his car is superior. I don't get it. Would this apply to scientists in a lab, working to cure cancer? Is a person playing badminton outside superior?

But rest assured that while I try to figure this out, I will be comfortably inside without an ounce of sweat on me, nothing crawling in my hair or down my shirt and reaching for a glass of iced tea that has nothing swimming in it.

Margaret Karmazin's credits include stories published in literary and national magazines, including *Rosebud, Chrysalis Reader, North Atlantic Review, Mobius, Confrontation, Pennsylvania Review, The Speculative Edge* and *Another Realm*. Her stories in *The MacGuffin, Eureka Literary Magazine, Licking River Review* and *Mobius* were nominated for Pushcart awards. Her story, "The Manly Thing," was nominated for the 2010 *Million Writers Award*. She has stories included in several anthologies, including *Still Going Strong, Ten Twisted Tales, Pieces of Eight (Autism Acceptance), Zero Gravity, Daughters of Icarus* and *Space Between Starts*. She has also published a YA novel, *Replacing Fiona* and a collection of short stories, *Risk*.

Jason Hackett

The Shoo Box

I found the pistol,

A .45 caliber revolver,

Wrapped in a newspaper

From the 1950s,

Stuffed deep in an

Old shoebox.

I heard it was one time

Used to clear up a

Back-alley brawl,

And another time used

To shoo away thugs

At the restaurant

Who were only thugs

Because of their skin.

You know rock, paper, scissors?

Well, oiled cloth beats metal

Every time

When rubbed against it

For sixty years straight,

Waiting for an

Opportunity to shine.

Jason Hackett is a small business owner, father of four and sleep deprived. His poems can be found in The Journal of American Poetry, Slippery Elm Literary Journal, Scarlet Leaf Review, Cholla Needles, Crack the Spine, Mental Papercuts, Blue River Review and Sky Island Journal.

Cathy Adams

Evangeline, The Blonde Bombshell

Evangeline Walker had a cut-out picture of Santa Claus on her wall, and right next to it was Carole Lombard and another was of Greta Garbo. My sister, Lucy, and I saw it through the front door when our Sunday School class went to her house to leave some apples at Christmastime. We figured out that she got them from the picture show house because our cousin Teddy said he sees her all the time sneaking around out back looking through the trash. Lots of people have pictures on their walls to keep the cold out but most people just use newspapers. Mama says Evangeline's a little bit off and that her real name is Evie, but she added all the rest of her name when she was in high school so she'd sound like a movie star. She's related to us somehow, a third cousin or something, but that describes most everybody in Looma, Alabama. Mama says all white people in Looma are blood related by at least a drop or two, but I can't see it because there's the Henchie family that lives over behind the sawmill. My sister and I both say we'd rather die than to think we're related to the Henchies. Their kids have lice and pinkeye all the time, and we know for a fact that Mrs. Henchie doesn't wear underwear, but I can't say how we know that. I guess if I had to pick between the Henchies and Evangeline to be related to, I'd pick Evangeline. When I told Mama that she just said, "Judge not lest ye be judged." She's always saying stuff like that, but I didn't think it made much sense since I figured I was complimenting Evangeline, and what I said about the Henchies was just the God's honest truth.

Mama had told us not to bother Evangeline because life had already been "tough enough on that poor girl." But there was something about her that was like picking at a scab. I just couldn't help myself. One night we followed Evangeline right to the movie theatre. Teddy was right about her going through the trash. She sneaked around to the rear of the building and sat behind a broken down wooden fence at the back of somebody's yard. Lucy and I waited on the other side of the street in the dark. Not long after, the picture show let out, and a few minutes after that they started turning off the lights out front. The fellow that runs the snack counter came out the backdoor carrying a big paper sack of leftover popped corn. He locked the door and dropped it in the trashcan. As soon as he peddled his bicycle down the street, Evangeline came out from behind the fence and went for that bag of popcorn. Lucy and I stepped out from where we'd been hiding like we were just passing by, and we walked right up to Evangeline. "Why hey there, Evangeline. It sure is a nice summer night for a walk." I shoved my hands in my pockets and rocked on my heels, trying to look the way I'd once seen a fellow do in a film.

Evangeline's eyes got wide. Her mouth was so full she could hardly talk. "Hey there."

"That popcorn looks so fresh and delicious. Lucy and I always have popcorn when we go to the picture show."

Evangeline swallowed hard and looked back and forth like she was expecting somebody. "Me too," she said, and suddenly her face changed and her voice went up higher. "I think it's divine to have popcorn when I'm watching Gary Cooper and Joan Leslie on the big screen." My sister, Lucy, started to laugh but I thumped her on the back of the head and made her stop. Before I could say anything else Evangeline started up again. "Now you girls need to get on home before your mama starts worrying about you. Only us adults are supposed to be out this time of night. Now go on, shoo." She made a little wave with her free hand, but she held tight to that big bag of popcorn with her other. I was a little peeved that she didn't offer us a taste.

Mama said Evangeline's parents died when she was a teenager, right about the time she changed her name. She has a younger brother who lives somewhere in Oklahoma. I've never seen him, and neither has Lucy. Mama said she'd seen him around town back before Mr. and Mrs. Walker died of the flu, just six days apart. All she said about him was that he had hair as red as a fire engine. I've never in my life seen anybody's hair the color of a fire engine, but Mama doesn't tell lies, so I guess walking around Oklahoma somewhere is a man with hair so red it hurts your eyes. Evangeline's hair was dark blonde like mine and my sister's. One time out in front of Pike's Grocery I heard Evangeline say that she wished her hair was as blonde as Jean Harlow's, the blonde bombshell. I saw a picture of Jean Harlow on the posters in front of the picture show and her hair was sure blonde. I figured if her hair could be that blonde then maybe Evangeline's brother's hair could be that red. I said Evangeline's hair *was* dark blonde like ours, because she did something that made the whole town talk about her. She disappeared for about a month and we all wondered if something had happened to her. The next thing you know she's walking around with hair that looked as blonde as Jean Harlow's except it wasn't fixed as nice like a movie star's. Evangeline's hair stuck up all over her head like it had been burned in places. She'd tie it up in little pieces of white cloth to try and make it curly and wavy, but she just looked like she had a mop on her head. We all laughed at her, but I made sure I didn't laugh right to her face. We heard some ladies at church saying that she must have stolen a bottle of bleach or something because everybody knew Evangeline hardly had a nickel to spend on stuff like hair color. Everybody said she'd steal stuff every chance she got. I heard one of Mama's friends say she once saw Evangeline stuffing a big napkin full of cornbread in her dress pocket at a funeral, and to steal at a funeral has got to be an extra bad sin.

Lucy and I got so curious we decided we'd ask Evangeline just what she'd done to her hair. I admit I was wondering about what it was like to have your hair colored. I even sneaked one of Mama's slips over my head in the bathroom and looked in the mirror trying to imagine what

I'd look like with white hair, but it just looked like underwear on my head so I stuffed it back in Mama's drawer before anyone knew. We showed up one Saturday morning at Evangeline's house, which really wasn't much of a house but a shack with cracks so big the bugs crawl inside to get warm in the winter and to cool off in the summer. Evangeline came to the door with half the little white rags missing from her hair. She was wearing a green dress that had been in fashion at least ten years earlier. I could see where she'd re-sewn the sleeves back in where they'd pulled loose. A button was missing from the front, and Evangeline had painted over a bottle cap with white paint and stuck it right where that button used to be. I could just make out the "RC" underneath the paint. I thought it was a really smart idea to use a bottle cap like that and I wanted to tell her so, but I just stood there trying to figure out how she'd made that cap stick in place.

"Hey there," said Evangeline. "I was just getting ready to go out."

"Yeah," I said, still looking at that bottle cap.

Evangeline's eyes narrowed a little bit and she put a hand over the bottle cap button. "I had to make some changes to the dress. It was Mama's."

I finally came to my senses and looked up at her face, "Uh, you look real pretty."

"Thank you." She gave us a little smile and looked down at my sister and then at me like she wanted us to leave but she was too nice to say so.

"We just wanted to ask you," I stopped. "We wanted to ask you a question."

Evangeline pulled another one of the little rags from her hair and tried to finger the fuzzy white hair into a curl. "Ask quick, now. I've got somewhere to be."

"How did you?" I scratched my head but then stopped quickly and dropped my hand. Mama always said if you scratch your head in public people will think you have lice. "We just wanted to know how you,

107

how you liked that Myrna Loy picture that's playing." Lucy punched my arm and I pushed her back a little. Evangeline stopped fooling around with those flimsy curls and tilted her head at me.

"I haven't got the chance to see that one yet. I've been busy."

"Yeah, well okay. We were just wondering. Bye." I grabbed my sister's hand and we hopped off her porch and started running. This time I didn't look back.

"Why didn't you ask about her hair?" whined Lucy when we finally stopped.

"I changed my mind," I snapped. The truth was I didn't really know why I didn't ask Evangeline about her hair except to say that when I saw her all dressed up in that tacky old green dress with her hair looking like a basket of cotton on her head, I knew something was up, something big.

"What do you mean you changed your mind? What for?" asked Lucy.

"She was getting all dolled up for something. I want to know for what?"

"Why'nt you go back and ask her?"

"You're so dumb, Lucy."

"I am not! You said you were going to ask her how her hair got all blonde like that, and you chickened out. You said you were going to ask. You're the one who's dumb," said Lucy.

My sister was eight years old, and most of the time she was as stupid as any other eight year old girl, but sometimes she got one up on me and I hated it when she did that. After all, I was twelve. I kicked at a stone in the road. "Just let me think a minute. I'm making a plan."

"What kinna plan?"

"The kinna plan you don't go blabbing to your little sister before you're ready." I squinted and tried to see what was happening back at Evangeline's house at the end of the road, but I couldn't see a thing.

She was up to something, all right. At first I reckoned she must have a date, but who would go on a date with Evangeline? She was nearly as old as my mama, and Mama was thirty years old. No woman thirty years old went on dates. The very idea was too crazy. It wasn't time for church, and Evangeline didn't go to our church anyway. She probably went to the church that the Henchies went to on the far side of town. A few women in Looma, like school teachers or the librarian or the lady who gives out car tags at the courthouse, get all dressed up to go to work, but this was four o'clock on a Friday afternoon, and nobody gets ready for work at that time of day, least of all Evangeline Walker.

The sun was still high when Evangeline finally came out of her house and started walking down the road toward town. I made Lucy get down low on the ground with me off the road until Evangeline passed. I wished I had on my overalls because the grass was itching my legs below my dress something fierce, and the sleeves were too tight over my elbows. I could hardly throw with that thing on, let alone hide in the bushes. Ever since my last birthday Mama had made me stop dressing up like a boy, and she cut up those overalls to use for rags. Watching Evangeline swishing down the road in that old dress, I couldn't for the life of me figure out why anybody would want to wear something as awful feeling as a dress when they could have been wearing overalls.

We let Evangeline get some distance before we started following her. Her hair wasn't sticking up the way it did before. It was flat against her head. From a distance, the dress looked a lot better. The hem was shorter than most women wore, but Evangeline was pretty tall for a woman. I figured her mother had been shorter than her and you can take a hem up, but you can let it down only so much. Evangeline was taking little steps like somebody trying to walk around baby chicks without mashing them. I couldn't see why she was having so much trouble walking on the road until we'd made it another mile and got into town. She was wearing white heels that looked like nursing shoes. If she could go through the trash at the picture show, then I guess she could sneak into the hospital and find herself a spare pair of nurse's shoes.

"What you reckon you'd look like in a dress like that?" asked Lucy, taking me by surprise.

I don't know why, but my face turned red, and I felt my hands sweating over the cotton floral flowers of my frock. "I reckon I'd look like a durn fool if you have to know."

"Lindy Blackmar says you need to take lessons to walk like a lady. She says you walk like a mule going to the feed barn at suppertime."

I walked faster, desperate to put some distance between myself and my big-mouthed sister. "I guess Lindy Blackmar can kiss my foot," I called over my shoulder. "And I wouldn't even bother to wash it first," I said even louder.

"Hey! Hey, where you reckon she's going?" Lucy ran to keep up, and soon she was huffing along beside me. "You think she's going to the picture show?"

"She ain't got the money to go to the picture show. And even if she did, why would she get all dressed up to do it?"

"Maybe she got herself a boyfriend," suggested Lucy.

"If she had a boyfriend then he'd be calling on her at home and driving her into town in his car." I thought a minute and then added, "Or at least he'd be walking with her into town."

We walked along in silence a few more minutes and Lucy said, "If I had a boyfriend he'd pick me up in a big car and bring me a box of chocolate candy."

I started to tell Lucy that she'd be lucky to have a boyfriend with a bicycle and a pack of gum, but suddenly up ahead, Evangeline turned and disappeared. I couldn't tell where she'd gone. I began to run and Lucy, now thoroughly hot and tired, cried out for me to slow down before she began a fast trot after me. I got half-way down the block where we'd seen Evangeline disappear and stopped. On that end of the street was a hardware store, an appliance shop that sold used ice boxes, stoves, and the like, and a tire and auto repair shop. She couldn't have gone into any of those places. I didn't figure a person like Evangeline needed any hardware. She sure couldn't afford an appliance even if it was used, and she didn't have a car that needed fixing. Then I spotted the sign.

Take your own professional portraits. Strips to tear and share. Ready in two minutes! 25 cents for 4 poses.

Lucy ran up behind me, all out of breath. "You didn't have to run off like that."

I was looking around the street, trying to figure out exactly where we were. Only one of the shops was still open, the auto repair place. I could see the backside of a man in the garage dressed in blue coveralls and making a racket with some kind of machine. When he stood up he scratched at the back of his head, and then I saw that he was a colored fellow. Lucy saw it, too, and her eyebrows went up at the sight. "Mama won't like this."

I pretended to be unconcerned. "Don't you want to find out what Evangeline's up to?" I pointed at the sign. Along the side of the words an arrow curved upward toward a set of stairs. The door was still open. Evangeline must have been in such a hurry she didn't bother pulling the door shut behind her.

Inside the stairwell, Lucy and I made shushing sounds at one another and then tip-toed up the stairs as quietly as we could creep. At the top was a hallway with some shops, small, run-down stores that didn't look like they did much business. A beauty parlor with pink faded letters that said *Racine's Beauty Shop* was shut down for the day. Next to that was a shop that sold hats, gloves, and scarves, also closed. A sign that read *Hal's Candies* brought a moment of excitement before we noticed the dust on the windows and the big lock on the door. Lucy pressed her face to the glass to see that the shelves had long since been emptied.

"Where is she?" Lucy whispered. Her voice echoed in the dismal hallway. "We've never been on this side of town before."

"I've been here a time or two," I said, but that was a lie. The place sure needed a good sweeping. At the end of the hall we heard a click and somebody said something, but we didn't catch what was said. It was Evangeline's voice.

The photo booth was pushed against the wall and there was hardly any light around it. A gray curtain was pulled shut over the place where a person sat down to get a picture made. The glow from the inside lit up Evangeline's white shoes and the bottom of her green skirt hanging over a low seat at the bottom. We walked with the quietest steps we knew, the steps we used when we didn't want Mama to hear us sneaking pie from the kitchen, and stopped in front of the photo booth. Lucy looked at me and I looked at her, and then we both looked back at the booth with Evangeline's green dress and feet showing. Over her knees the edges of the dress hung ragged with little strings from where she'd pulled the hem out as low as it would go.

The click sounded, followed by a cuss word I can't repeat. Lucy gasped and put a hand over her mouth. I put a finger to my lips warning her to keep quiet. We were both sure Evangeline must have heard the noise, but the man in the auto shop outside was still making noise with that machine, so I guess between that and her being so caught up in the picture making, Evangeline didn't notice us at all.

I had a plan. I got down on all fours and crawled until my head was nearly at the bottom of the booth's curtain. It wasn't easy with my skirt hanging in the way, but then I rolled over onto my back and pushed with my feet so that I could see up into the booth. I was expecting Evangeline to look down at any second and start screaming and we'd all get a big laugh, but she had her face all smushed up in this funny expression with her hand in front of her mouth and she was looking right at the thing on the wall that made the picture. When the camera clicked she made a blow-a-kiss motion with her hand, but she must have gotten the timing wrong, because she said that cuss word again. I was just about to pull my head back out, but that was when she spotted my face down at her feet and she jumped up from her seat. It was in that second when she first looked down that the camera clicked for the last time. She jerked the curtain back and saw Lucy down on her hands and knees giggling so hard I thought she'd pee her pants. I jumped back up onto my knees.

"What do you two think you're doing?!" She was so mad tears spilled from her eyes. Her face looked as if it would burst open like a melon.

"We were just funning you, Evangeline," I said, trying to calm her down.

"Funning me? What for? Can't you see I'm trying to do something important?"

A strand of hair had fallen down over one of Evangeline's eyes and stuck in her tears. I shushed at Lucy behind me, but it didn't do any good.

"You're just getting pictures made," I said.

"You wouldn't understand!" She wiped away her tears. Her eyes were puffy and her skin was so pink from crying, I couldn't help think of a baby opossum I'd once seen.

I stood up from the floor, and something made me want to straighten out the front of my now dirty and wrinkled dress. "I got my picture made at school."

"These pictures were for a modeling agency, if it's any of your business!" she hissed. "If you send them your picture, a place in Memphis takes on girls and they get jobs in Hollywood in the movies. Why do you think I swept the floors for nothing at that beauty parlor for three whole weeks to get my hair done? Huh?"

For a second I didn't know what to say, and Lucy's stifled giggles were the only sound. "We didn't know you worked in a beauty parlor."

"Well I did! And now my pictures are ruined because of you."

"Just the last one."

"I only needed one," she shrieked.

"Why don't you make another set?"

"Because that was my last quarter! The very last one!" On that last word she ran right out of the booth and down the stairs, leaving her pictures lying in the dispenser. I stood there staring at the stairs Evangeline had stomped down, feeling something hard in my stomach that made me sick inside. Clasping my arms around myself, I looked down at my legs, streaked with dust, and my scuffed brown shoes. Lucy had stopped her laughing when Evangeline ran off, and she came closer, looking up at me quietly, waiting for me to explain something I knew I had no words for. In a minute the last picture strip rolled into the dispenser. In the first picture Evangeline's eyes were closed, and in the next two her hand lay palm up in front of her face in a kiss blown too late. The last tiny square was of her looking down at something unseen, her white hair covering part of her face, and her eyes, angry and hopeless.

Cathy Adams' latest novel, *A Body's Just as Dead*, was released in 2018 by *SFK Press*. Her writing has been nominated twice for a Pushcart Prize. She is a short story writer with stories published in *Utne, AE: The Canadian Science Fiction Review, Barely South, A River and Sound Review, Upstreet, Southern Pacific Review,* and 45 other journals from around the world. She earned her M.F.A. at Rainier Writing Workshop, Pacific Lutheran University, Washington. She lives and writes in Liaoning, China, with her husband, photographer, Julian Jackson.

Adrienne Krater

Steeping Cellos in Rosemary Oil

My mother told me I would get tired of it, just like when I decided I didn't like the piano anymore. I leaned over the kitchen countertop, my belly pressing into the edge, and my hands folded in a prayer in front of me. I said I really needed to play the violin, not the piano. I would practice the violin I said, because it wasn't boring like the piano. My mother leaned over a steamy pot, stirring marshmallows and puffed riced with both of her hands gripping the wooden spoon. She looked over at her daughter, prostrate on the kitchen counter, and sighed.

A professor once told me that he used peppermint oil for deodorant. His Aunt gave him a bottle, while mumbling something about antiperspirants and cancer. He told me he didn't know how concentrated the oil was, and he shook the bottle until a pool of peppermint was cradled in the palm of his hand. He slapped the peppermint onto the desired area, and the potent oils began to burn his skin. The recommended amount of oil to be used as a deodorant is one drop.

I was reading eighth notes to my mother. My feet were thrown up onto the dashboard of the 94' S-Series Saturn, my toes pressing against the glass of the windshield. It made my toes cold.

My mother sat down on the worn living room carpet by my feet. She pulled out a small glass bottle and unscrewed the lid. She said it was cedarwood, and she poured some into her hand and began to rub it onto the bottoms of my size 4 feet. My mother was going on about how the oil would interact with my brain, seeping into the pineal gland. It would help release the body's natural sleeping hormone, melatonin, allowing me sleep more soundly. My father said it was probably psychosomatic. My mother rolled her eyes. My feet tingled, and a thick, clean wooden scent hung in the air.

I wiggled in the wooden chair, its spindled back digging into my kidneys. The music sheets in front of me still looked foreign, and I was growing impatient. I rested my chin onto the plastic rest, and lifted the bow to the strings. Notes fell off the strings, but never came alive. There was too much of a break in between every note as I scooted forward to squint at the notes and count FACE before I could begin the next measure. My mother called that dinner was ready, and I stumbled down the stairs, my socks slipping on their edges. As I stirred my mashed potatoes and turnips together, I saw a small sprig of green caught under a piece of carrot. I plucked it out, and my mother noted that she had left the rosemary in for color, but that we shouldn't eat it, because it would taste bitter.

My mother told me a story I had never heard the other day. She said I was about three, and I had been ill for months. She said they took me from doctor to doctor, and each one shook his or her head and drummed their fingers on their clipboards. Finally, my mother laid me down onto my bed, and pulled out a small cotton bag. She pulled out a glass bottle labeled "oregano", and wiggled the pink socks off of my feet. The oregano smelled like Italian sausage pasta grease. She said she had read in a book somewhere that it could help unknown illnesses. She began to rub it on my feet, and at first nothing happened. Then she told me that my little fists began to grip the blankets, and I began to tremble. I gagged, and rolled onto my side, white foam spilling out of my mouth. I continued to throw up the foam for several minutes, and my mother held me to her chest as I threw up over her shoulder. I spit out the last bit, and fell back onto the sheets. I pulled down my sleeve and wiped it across my mouth.

"How do you feel?" she asked.

"Better." I nodded and asked if we could have chocolate chip pancakes for dinner.

It smelled like sweat and rotting roses in our room. I sat at my desk with my back to my roommate's back at her desk. We were a mirror. Stretching my arms into the air, I wiggled my fingers and mentioned that we should buy an aromatherapy diffuser. Orange blossom mixed with cloves and peppermint soon began to seep into our lungs and blankets. I threw out the flowers above my desk. A few days later I sat in my room, chair facing out, and cello placed firmly between my legs. The edges of the cello dug into the insides of my knees, and the neck rested on my left shoulder.

Lemongrass spilled out of the diffuser on my dresser, and my thoughts ran everywhere but on the music sheets in front of me. I thought about my paper on John Donne's metaphysical poetry. I thought about the boy I had just started dating. I wondered whether it was snowing outside. It was. I wondered if I was pre- or a- millennial. I still didn't know. I lifted the bow to the strings and squinted at the notes as I pulled the horsehairs across the ribbed wire. It dripped molasses tones, and it began to feel too warm in the room. I could feel my face pulsing. I can't sweat, so my body overheats in a very short amount of time. I laid the bow down and lifted my hand to my cheek. It was hot under the cool pads of my fingers. Resting the cello onto the floor, I walked over to the window. I opened the window and let the cool breeze fill and tumble through the room. My skin cooled and I smelled ice and bark in the air. I stood in front of the window with my arms on the sill, and my nose pressed to the screen.

I figured I would probably give up on this as well. Turning off the diffuser, I put the cello into my closet, and began to unclasp the screen from the window. My fingers trembled as they pulled on the metal tabs at the edges the window. I know I could have closed the window, sat back down, and kept practicing, but running away from hard things had become so comforting. So I pushed the loosened screen onto the snow and swung through the window. I ran across the powdered grass, and jogged in my socks until my toes felt soggy and brittle. I collapsed under a tree and let the snow begin to soak through my sweatpants. My sweater had slipped over my shoulder, and I pulled it back up into place. It slid back off my shoulder. I ground my teeth together and pulled my knees to my chest. I stared at a sprig of pine browning in the snow for a few minutes. I realized with a pang that I could still smell lemongrass on my skin and clothes. I could still smell the lemongrass. I stood up quickly. I jogged back to the dorm, ignoring the numb buzz beginning to creep through my toes. I crawled back through the window and threw open the closet door. I pulled out the cello and pressed it into dimples on the insides of my knees. I closed my eyes and saw rosemary oil spilling down the sides the cello, slipping into the sound hole, pooling around the bottom, seeping into the wood. I opened my eyes and picked up the bow. I looked down at the music. I still couldn't read the measure. I drew the bow across the wires. It still sounded tired and bored. I decided I would have to steep the cello in the oil. I closed my eyes again.

Adrienne Krater is a published writer and undergraduate student in the International Studies program at Cedarville University. She works as a university and professional photographer. She is from Altoona, Pennsylvania.

Cheyenne Avila

Brujeria and Bonnets: A Brown Girl's Guide to Decolonization and Self-Actualization

It's past midnight, and I'm trying to convince myself to masturbate

under the guise of "self-love" or "anxiety-release", but,

really,

the act is more habitual and shameful than it is pleasuring, and,

really,

I'm just tired

and wish I had someone else to do it for me. So,

I lie flat on my back and adjust my bonnet around my ears and

place the ghost of a man's head between my thighs and

conjure the song I want him to sing into me and

I clutch the crystals on my chest because

I can feel the spirits pulsing in the room and

the song I'm making up doesn't have lyrics but

it's a nice melody that I can't remember until

I need to hum another orgasm out of myself, and

now, I imagine the earth of my chest crumbling into

the hands of an exhaling nebula, and

I remember that I read somewhere that brujeria

is about entering an interaction with the living universe, and

this belief stems from the Aztecs, so,

maybe touching myself is a form of resistance   or

is a testament to legacy   or

energy   or

spirituality   or

maybe I am a brown woman learning to be alone.

To fall into the reserves of myself and

rely on my own strength to keep me upright,

to tilt my face towards the sun,

to smile at nothing and everything,

to frown at white men who stare at my legs for too long,

to frown at brown men who stare at my hair for too long,

to stop frowning at myself.

Or,   maybe masturbation is forgiveness.

Is me wanting myself for the first time,

owning my body for the first time and

watching my body listen to me,

seeing my body crumbling into my own hands and

I am limitless,

lying on my back and feeling my body beneath me,

just a casing for my spirit,

and my spirit,

taking up the space of this entire room,

touching the particles of light and dissolving,

over and over

until I have mastered this movement,

until I have sated the hunger,

relinquished the burning, and

commanded me back to myself.

Cheyenne Avila is an Afromexicana competitive Slam Poet from Bellflower, California. She has had a nonfiction essay published by the University of La Verne's *Prism Review*. Her writing centers around experience, identity, race, womanhood, and spirituality.

Robert Laughlin

Men At Work: Dion, a Contractor

I can't imagine building a house I wouldn't live in myself. Textured paint is standard for our interior walls, but unless a customer specifically asks for ceilings to match, we do something else: panels, planks and beams, popcorn, you name it. I lived in a house with a textured ceiling for two years, and it was awful. Since high school, not a day has passed that I'm not worried about my family or my business. Those worries are with me from the time I open my eyes in the morning, and for two years, I started the day with a Rorschach test, seeing all kinds of nasty things take shape overhead in the dawn light.

Robert Laughlin lives in Chico, California, and received his BA at California State University, Sacramento. In addition to his continuing "Men at Work" series, he has published 100 short stories, mostly flash length; two of his longer stories are *storySouth Million Writers Award Notable Stories*. He has also published 200 poems, and his last publication in *Crack the Spine* was his poem, "Sowing Seeds of Wheat," in Issue Fifty-Eight.

www.ingramcontent.com/pod-product-compliance
Lightning Source LLC
Chambersburg PA
CBHW020626250626
47154CB00004B/1695